W9-CJP-120

Flags *of the* World

A Comprehensive Guide

Flags of the World

A Comprehensive Guide

Published by PRC Publishing Ltd.
Kiln House, 210 New Kings Road,
London SW6 4NZ

Published in the USA in 1995 and reprinted in 1998,
by JG Press. Distributed by World Publications, Inc.

The JG Press imprint is a trademark of
JG Press, Inc.
455 Somerset Avenue
North Dighton, MA 02764

Flags authenticated by the Flag Research Center
Winchester, Massachusetts, Mass 01890 USA

ISBN 1 57215 092 0

Printed and bound in China

Contents

United Nations

Computer Cartography by AND Map Graphics Ltd., Finchampstead, Berkshire.

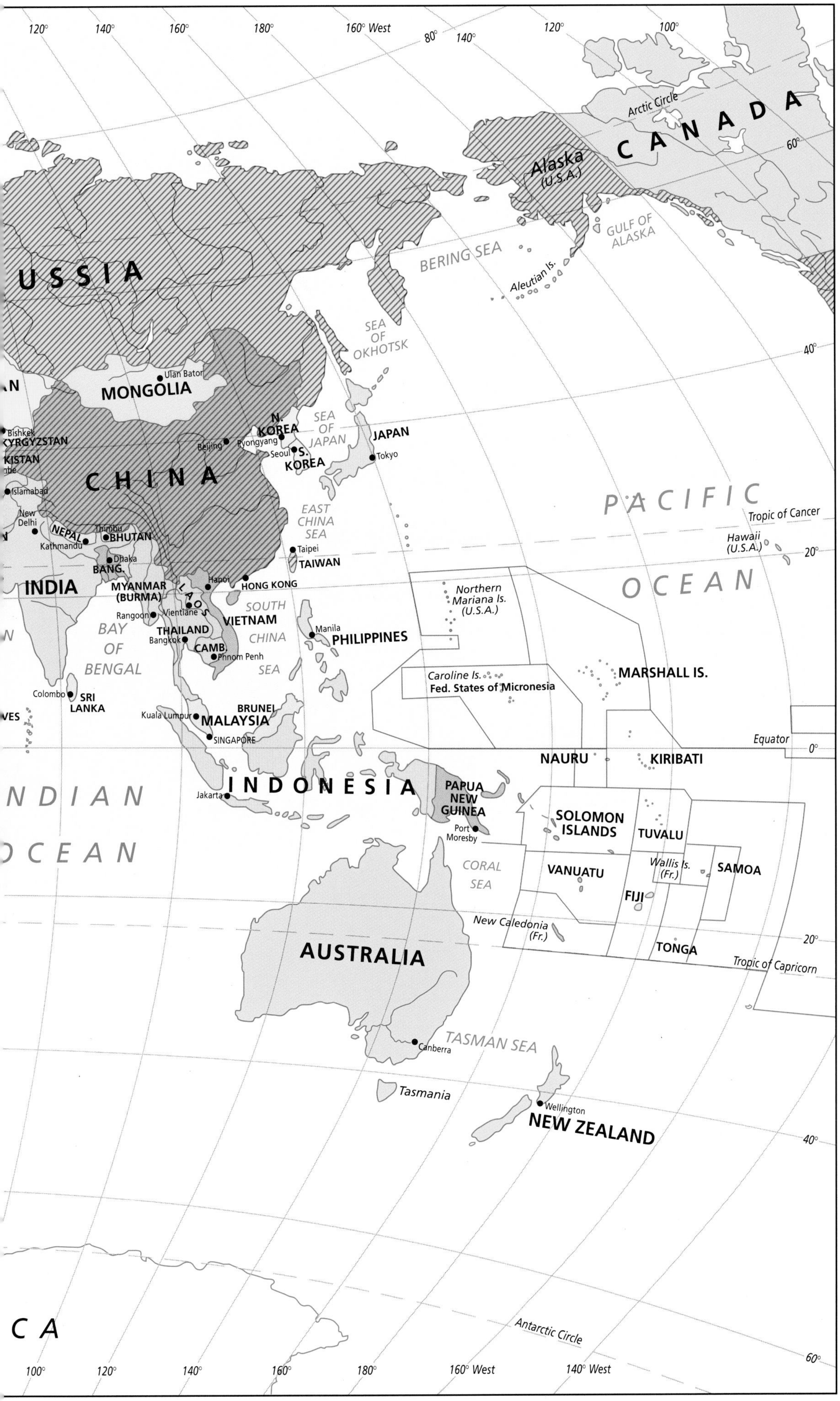

KEY

- 1945 (Founder Member)
- 1946-56
- 1957-67
- 1968-78
- Since 1979
- Country with observer status
- Permanent member of security councill

Western Sahara-administered by Morocco

ALB.	-Albania
AUS.	-Austria
BANG.	-Bangladesh
BEL.	-Belgium
BOS.	-Bosnia-Herzegovina
BUL.	-Bulgaria
CAMB.	-Cambodia
DOM.REP.	-Dominican Republic
E.G.	-Equatorial Guinea
HUNG.	-Hungary
JORD.	-Jordan
LEB.	-Lebanon
LUX.	-Luxembourg
MAC.	-Macedonia
NETH.	-Netherlands
ROM.	-Romania
RUS.	-Russia
S.	-Slovenia
SLOVAK.	-Slovak Republic
SUR.	-Suriname
SWZ.	-Switzerland
U.A.E.	-United Arab Emirates
YUGO.	-Yugoslavia

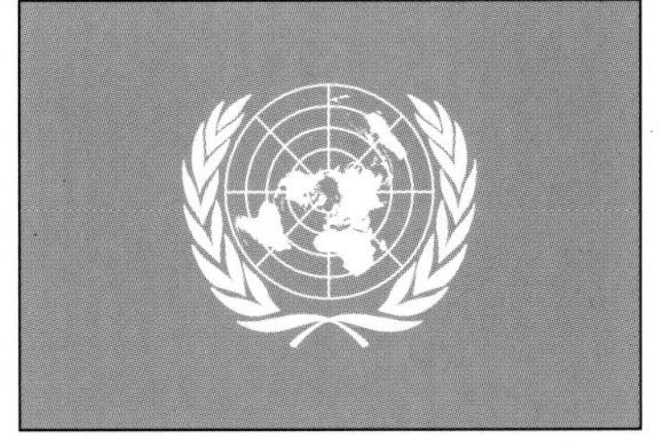

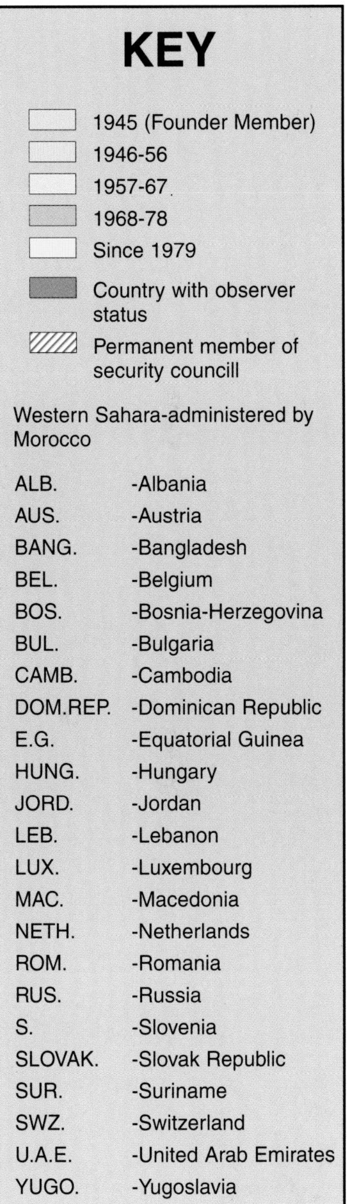

Flags of Europe

EUROPE FLAG INDEX

Flags of Europe

ALBANIA

Facts and Figures

Capital: Tirana 251,000 (1990)
Area (sq km): 28,748
Population: 3,300,000 (1991)
Language: Albanian, Greek, English
Religion: Sunni Muslim 70% Orthodox 20%
Roman Catholic 10%
Currency: Lek = 100 quindars
Annual Income per person: $1,000
Annual Trade per person: $73
Adult Literacy: 85%
Life Expectancy (F): 75
Life Expectancy (M): 70

Location Map

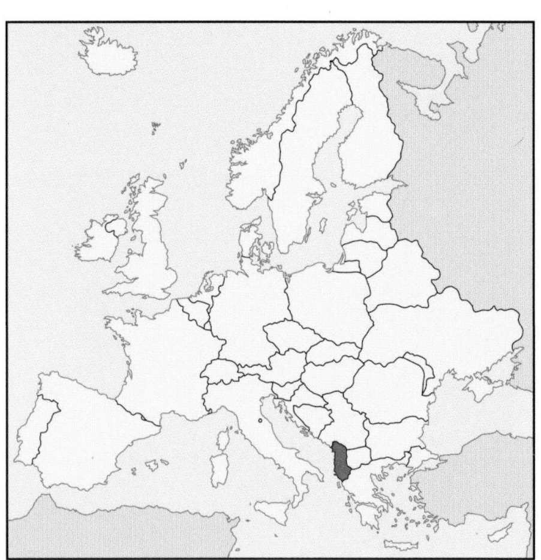

ANDORRA

Facts and Figures

Capital: Andorra la vella 19,000 (1990)
Area (sq km): 453
Population: 59,000 (1993)
Language: Catalan, Spanish, French
Religion: Roman Catholic
Currency: French Franc, Spanish Peseta
Annual Income per person: $14,000
Annual Trade per person: $9,000
Adult Literacy: Data not available
Life Expectancy (F): 81
Life Expectancy (M): 74

Location Map

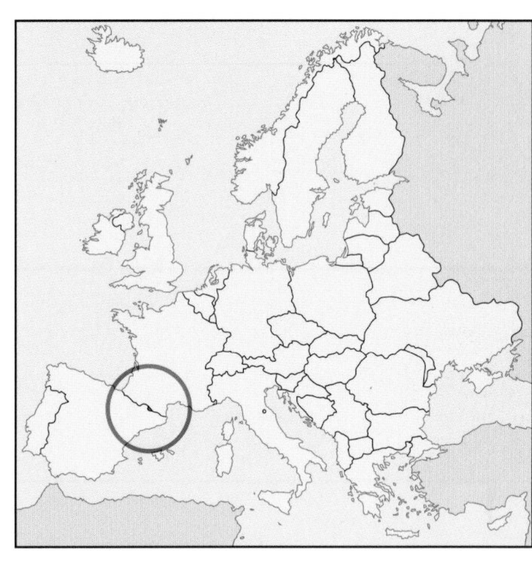

AUSTRIA

Facts and Figures

Capital: Vienna 1,539,850 (1991)
Area (sq km): 83,860
Population: 7,800,000 (1991)
Language: German
Religion: Roman Catholic 78% Protestant 5%
Currency: Schilling = 100 groschen
Annual Income per person: $20,380
Annual Trade per person: $11,653
Adult Literacy: 99%
Life Expectancy (F): 79
Life Expectancy (M): 72

Location Map

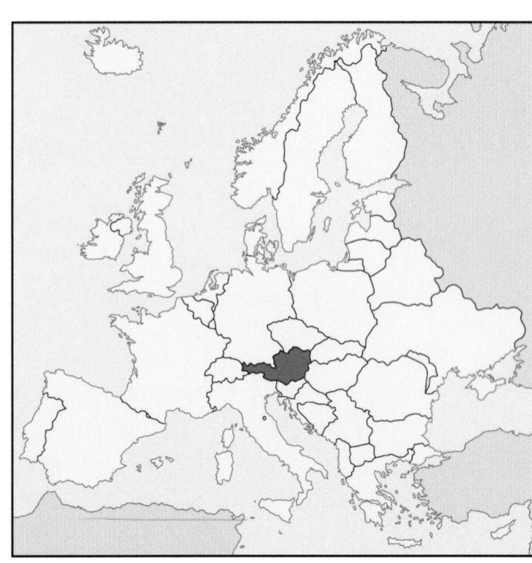

BELARUS

Facts and Figures

Capital: Minsk 1,613,000 (1990)
Area (sq km): 207,600
Population: 10,280,000 (1992)
Language: Belorussian, Russian
Religion: Christian Orthodox, Roman Catholic
Currency: Rouble
Annual Income per person: $3,110
Annual Trade per person: $1,000
Adult Literacy: 95%
Life Expectancy (F): 75
Life Expectancy (M): 64

Location Map

BELGIUM

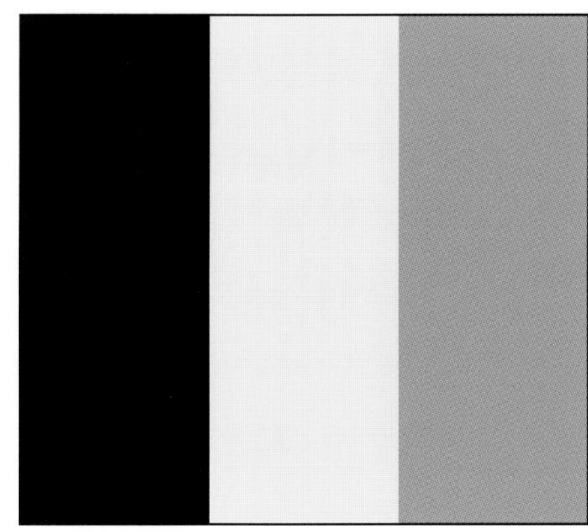

Facts and Figures

Capital: Brussels 1,331,000 (1991)
Area (sq km): 30,530
Population: 10,020,000 (1992)
Language: Flemish, Dutch, Walloon
Religion: Roman Catholic 72% Protestant
Currency: Belgian Franc
Annual Income per person: $19,300
Annual Trade per person: $23,443
Adult Literacy: 99%
Life Expectancy (F): 79
Life Expectancy (M): 72

Location Map

BOSNIA-HERZEGOVINA

Facts and Figures

Capital: Sarajevo 526,000 (1991)
Area (sq km): 51,129
Population: 4,366,000 (1991)
Language: Serbo-Croat
Religion: Muslim 40% Orthodox 31%
Roman Catholic 15%
Currency: Dinar
Annual Income per person: $3,000
Annual Trade per person: $900
Adult Literacy: 86%
Life Expectancy (F): 73
Life Expectancy (M): 68

Location Map

Flags of Europe

BULGARIA

Facts and Figures

Capital: Sofia 1,141,140 (1990)
Area (sq km): 110,994
Population: 8,470,000 (1992)
Language: Bulgarian, Turkish, Romany
Religion: Eastern Orthodox 80%
Sunni Muslim
Currency: Lev = 100 stotinki
Annual Income per person: $1,840
Annual Trade per person: $2,000
Adult Literacy: 93%
Life Expectancy (F): 76
Life Expectancy (M): 70

Location Map

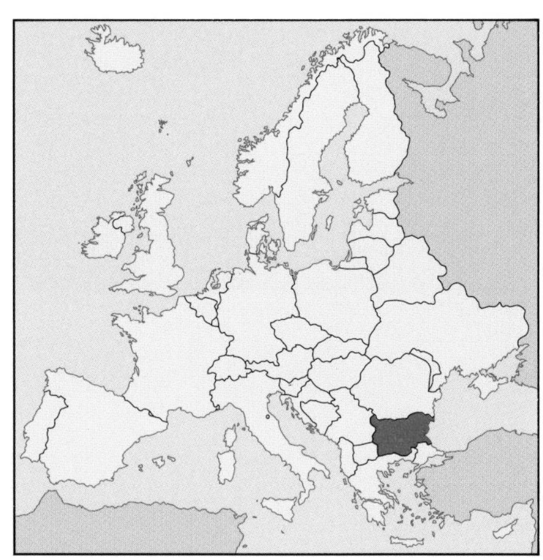

CROATIA

Facts and Figures

Capital: Zagreb 726,770 (1991)
Area (sq km): 56,540
Population: 4,790,000 (1992)
Language: Serbo-Croat
Religion: Roman Catholic 77% Orthodox 11%
Currency: Croatian Dinar
Annual Income per person: $5,600
Annual Trade per person: $1,500
Adult Literacy: 96%
Life Expectancy (F): 74
Life Expectancy (M): 67

Location Map

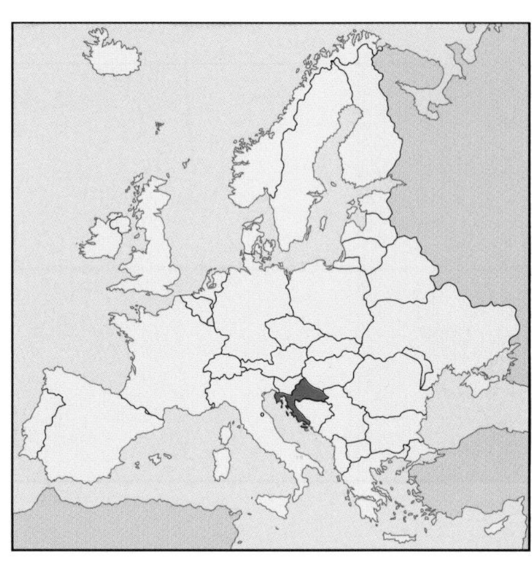

CYPRUS

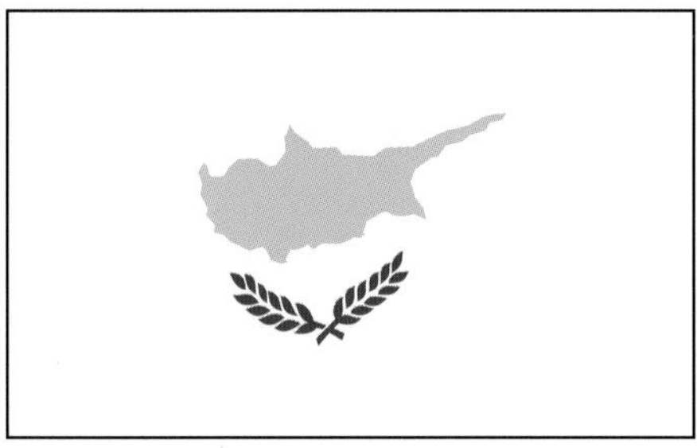

Facts and Figures

Capital: Nicosia 166,500 (1991)
Area (sq km): 9,250
Population: 725,000 (1994)
Language: Greek, Turkish, English
Religion: Greek Orthodox 79% Muslim 18%
Currency: Cyprus Pound
Annual Income per person: $8,640
Annual Trade per person: $5,032
Adult Literacy: 94%
Life Expectancy (F): 79
Life Expectancy (M): 74

Location Map

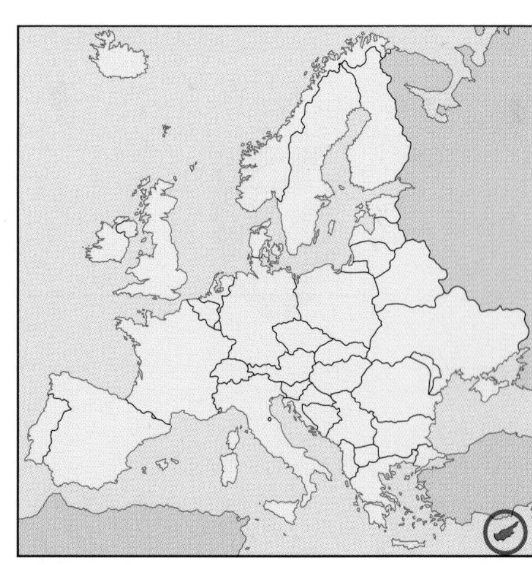

CZECH REPUBLIC

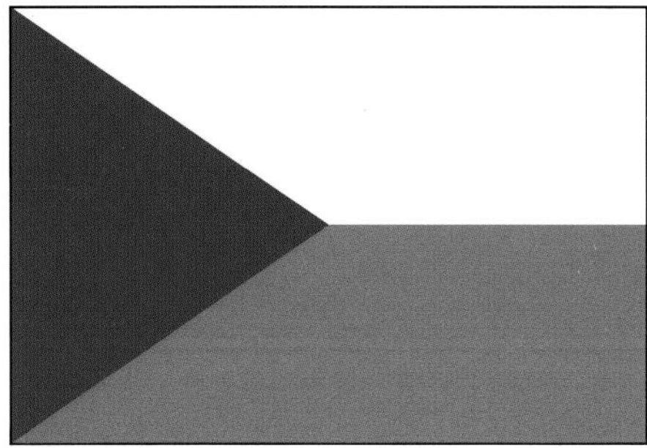

Facts and Figures

Capital: Prague 1,120,000 (1990)
Area (sq km): 79,000
Population: 10,330,000 (1993)
Language: Czech
Religion: Protestant
Currency: Koruna = 100 halura
Annual Income per person: Data not available
Annual Trade per person: Data not available
Adult Literacy: 99%
Life Expectancy (F): 76
Life Expectancy (M): 69

Location Map

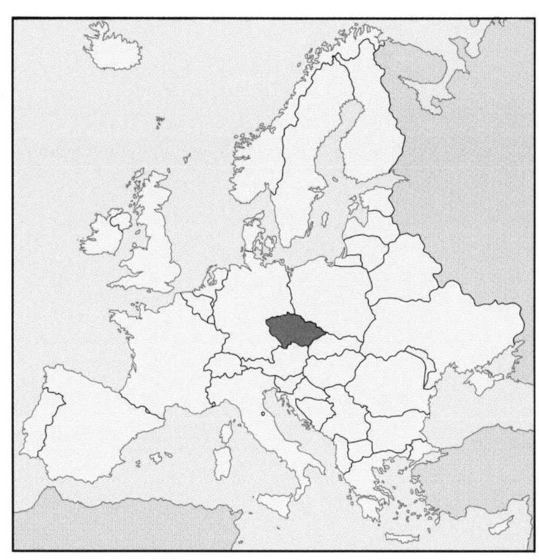

DENMARK

Facts and Figures

Capital: Copenhagen 1,342,680 (1993)
Area (sq km): 43,075
Population: 5,180,000 (1993)
Language: Danish
Religion: Lutheran 90%
Currency: Krone = 100 øre
Annual Income per person: $23,660
Annual Trade per person: $14,046
Adult Literacy: 99%
Life Expectancy (F): 79
Life Expectancy (M): 73

Location Map

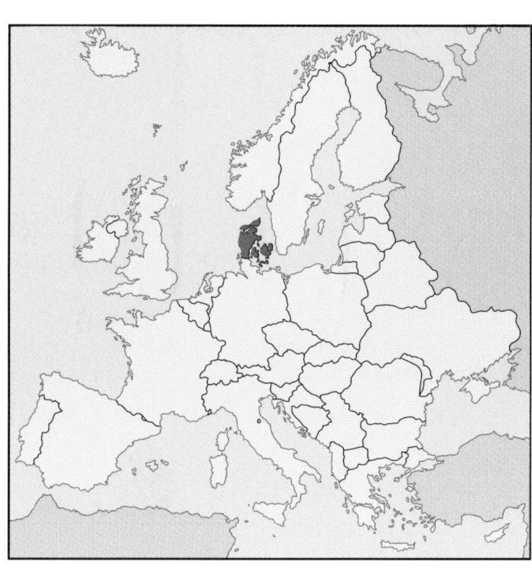

ESTONIA

Facts and Figures

Capital: Tallinn 502,400 (1991)
Area (sq km): 45,100
Population: 1,600,000 (1992)
Language: Estonian, Russian
Religion: Lutheran, Orthodox
Currency: Kroon = 100 sents
Annual Income per person: $3,830
Annual Trade per person: $850
Adult Literacy: Data not available
Life Expectancy (F): 75
Life Expectancy (M): 66

Location Map

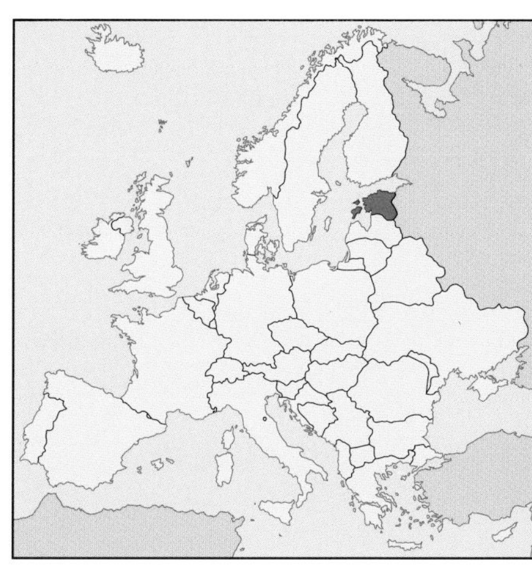

Flags of Europe

FINLAND

Facts and Figures

Capital: Helsinki 501,500 (1992)
Area (sq km): 338,100
Population: 5,050,000 (1992)
Language: Finnish, Swedish
Religion: Lutheran 87%
Currency: Markka = 100 penniä
Annual Income per person: $21,009
Annual Trade per person: $8,852
Adult Literacy: 99%
Life Expectancy (F): 80
Life Expectancy (M): 72

Location Map

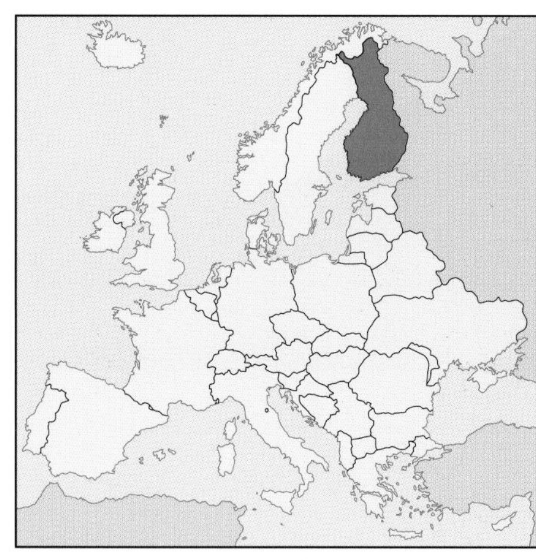

FRANCE

Facts and Figures

Capital: Paris 9,318,800 (1990)
Area (sq km): 543,965
Population: 57,800,000 (1994)
Language: French
Religion: Roman Catholic 73%
Other Christian 4% Muslim 3%
Currency: Franc = 100 centimes
Annual Income per person: $20,600
Annual Trade per person: $8,195
Adult Literacy: 99%
Life Expectancy (F): 81
Life Expectancy (M): 73

Location Map

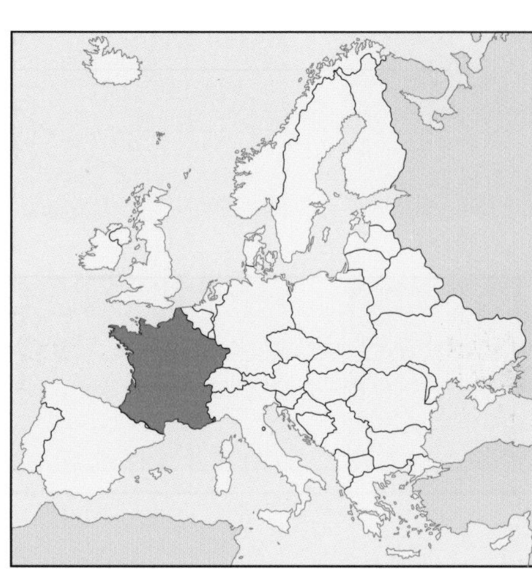

GERMANY

Facts and Figures

Capital: Berlin 3,437,900 (1990)
Area (sq km): 356,700
Population: 80,280,000 (1992)
Language: German
Religion: Protestant 45% Roman Catholic 35%
Currency: Deutschmark = 100 pfennig
Annual Income per person: $23,650
Annual Trade per person: $12,860
Adult Literacy: 99%
Life Expectancy (F): 78
Life Expectancy (M): 72

Location Map

GREECE

Facts and Figures

Capital: Athens 3,096,800 (1991)
Area (sq km): 131,960
Population: 10,260,000 (1991)
Language: Greek
Religion: Greek Orthodox 98%
Currency: Drachma = 100 lepta
Annual Income per person: $6,374
Annual Trade per person: $3,005
Adult Literacy: 93%
Life Expectancy (F): 79
Life Expectancy (M): 74

Location Map

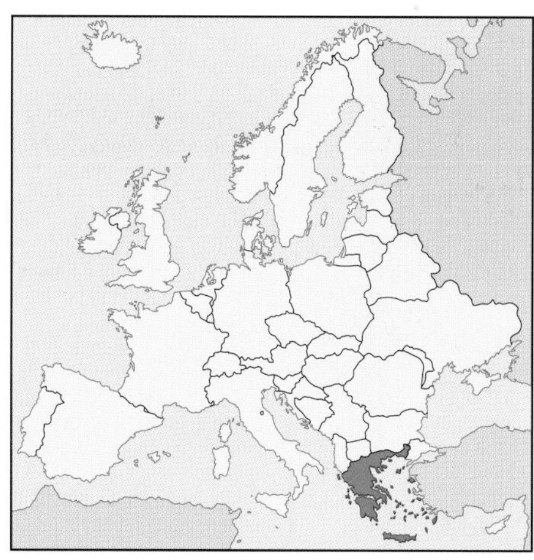

HUNGARY

Facts and Figures

Capital: Budapest 2,016,000 (1992)
Area (sq km): 93,030
Population: 10,310,000 (1993)
Language: Hungarian, Slovak, German
Religion: Roman Catholic 68% Protestant 25%
Currency: Forint = 100 filler
Annual Income per person: $2,690
Annual Trade per person: $2,109
Adult Literacy: 99%
Life Expectancy (F): 75
Life Expectancy (M): 68

Location Map

ICELAND

Facts and Figures

Capital: Reykjavik 100,850 (1992)
Area (sq km): 103,000
Population: 262,190 (1992)
Language: Icelandic
Religion: Lutheran 92%
Currency: Króna = 100 aurar
Annual Income per person: $24,570
Annual Trade per person: $12,592
Adult Literacy: 99%
Life Expectancy (F): 81
Life Expectancy (M): 75

Location Map

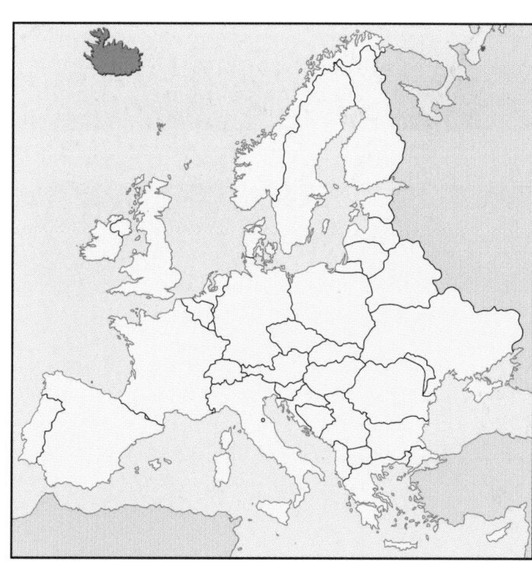

Flags of Europe

IRELAND

Facts and Figures

Capital: Dublin 915,516 (1991)
Area (sq km): 70,280
Population: 3,550,000 (1992)
Language: Irish, English
Religion: Roman Catholic 90% Protestant 3%
Currency: Punt = 100 pence
Annual Income per person: $10,780
Annual Trade per person: $14,305
Adult Literacy: 99%
Life Expectancy (F): 78
Life Expectancy (M): 73

Location Map

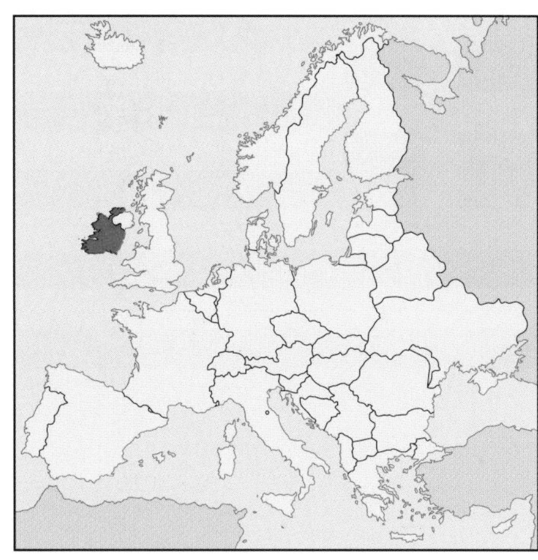

ITALY

Facts and Figures

Capital: Rome 2,723,330 (1992)
Area (sq km): 301,300
Population: 56,960,000 (1992)
Language: Italian
Religion: Roman Catholic 84%
Currency: Lira
Annual Income per person: $18,580
Annual Trade per person: $6,192
Adult Literacy: 97%
Life Expectancy (F): 80
Life Expectancy (M): 73

Location Map

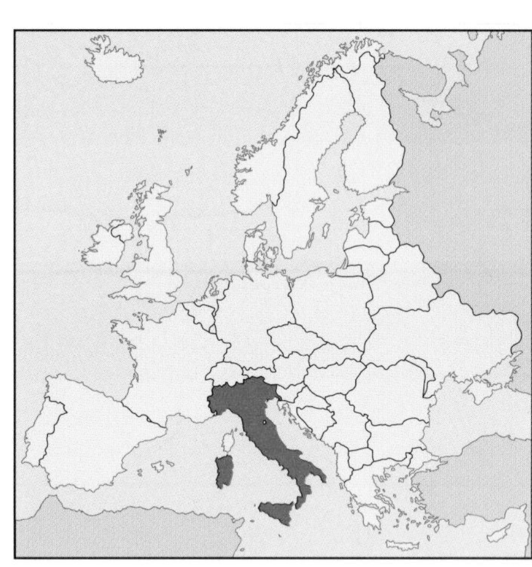

LATVIA

Facts and Figures

Capital: Riga 910,200 (1991)
Area (sq km): 63,700
Population: 2,610,000 (1993)
Language: Latvian, Russian
Religion: Lutheran
Currency: Lat = 100 santims
Annual Income per person: $3,410
Annual Trade per person: $3,400
Adult Literacy: Data not available
Life Expectancy (F): 75
Life Expectancy (M): 64

Location Map

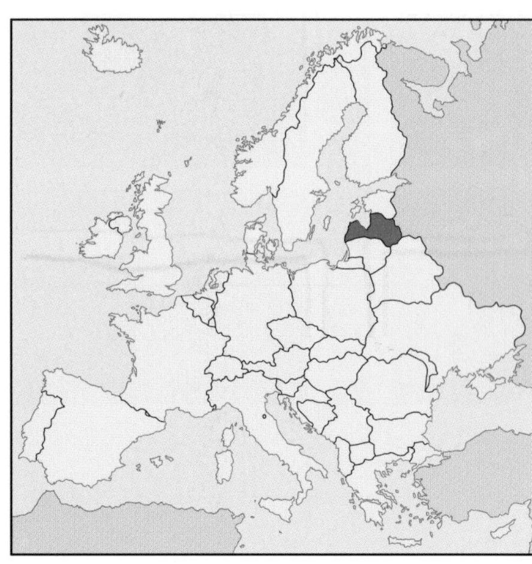

LIECHTENSTEIN

Facts and Figures

Capital: Vaduz 4,870 (1990)
Area (sq km): 160
Population: 29,800 (1992)
Language: German
Religion: Roman Catholic 85% Protestant 8%
Currency: Swiss Franc = 100 centines
Annual Income per person: $33,000
Annual Trade per person: Data not available
Adult Literacy: 99%
Life Expectancy (F): 81
Life Expectancy (M): 73

Location Map

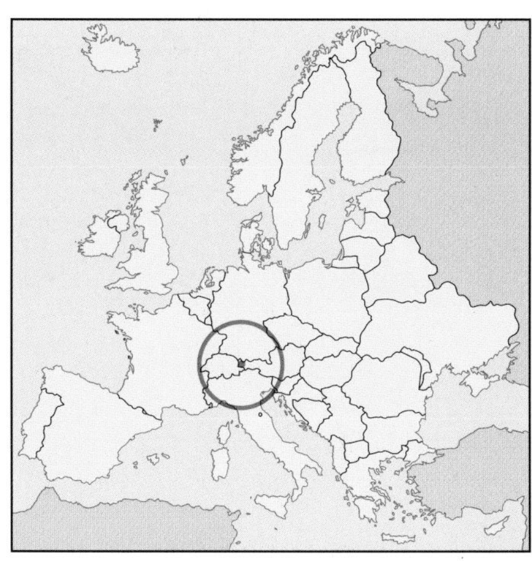

LITHUANIA

Facts and Figures

Capital: Vilnius 592,500 (1990)
Area (sq km): 65,200
Population: 3,740,000 (1994)
Language: Lithuanian, Russian
Religion: Roman Catholic 90% Lutheran
Currency: Litas = 100 centas
Annual Income per person: $2,710
Annual Trade per person: Data not available
Adult Literacy: Data not available
Life Expectancy (F): 76
Life Expectancy (M): 66

Location Map

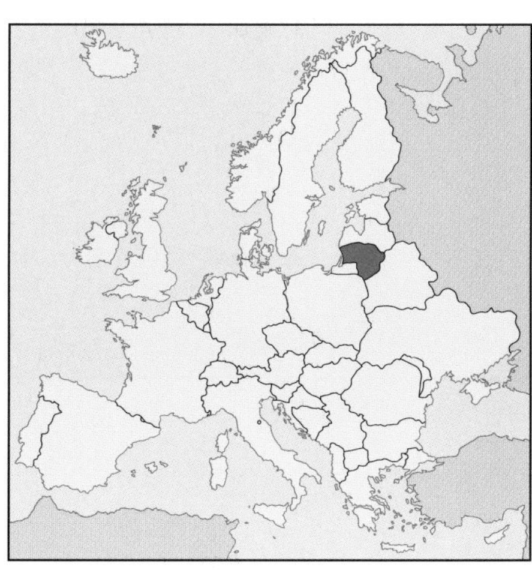

LUXEMBOURG

Facts and Figures

Capital: Luxembourg 75,377 (1991)
Area (sq km): 2,590
Population: 395,200 (1993)
Language: Letzeburgish, French, German
Religion: Roman Catholic 95%
Currency: Luxembourg Franc = 100 centimes
Annual Income per person: $31,080
Annual Trade per person: $35,000
Adult Literacy: 100%
Life Expectancy (F): 79
Life Expectancy (M): 72

Location Map

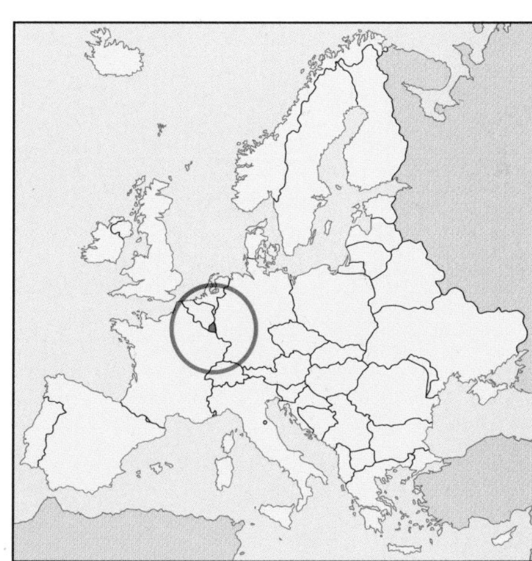

Flags of Europe

MACEDONIA

Facts and Figures

Capital: Skopje 448,230 (1991)
Area (sq km): 25,700
Population: 2,060,000 (1992)
Language: Macedonian, Albanian
Religion: Orthodox 67% Muslim 30%
Currency: Dinar = 100 deni
Annual Income per person: $3,100
Annual Trade per person: $800
Adult Literacy: 89%
Life Expectancy (F): 72
Life Expectancy (M): 68

Location Map

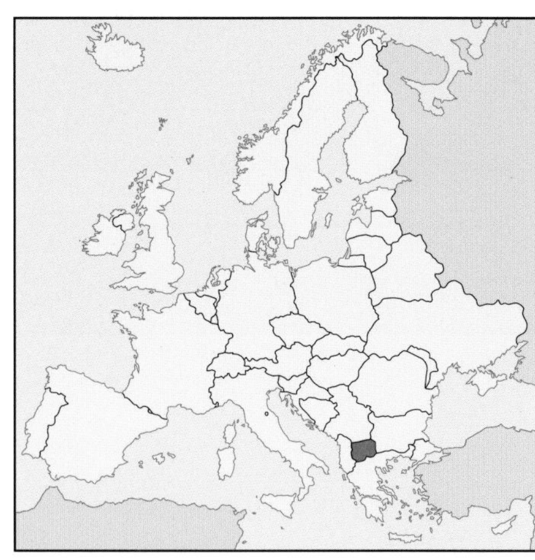

MALTA

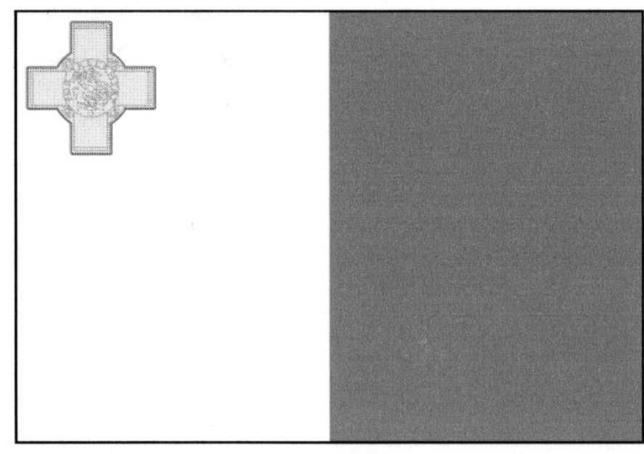

Facts and Figures

Capital: Valletta 101,750 (1990)
Area (sq km): 316
Population: 364,600 (1993)
Language: Maltese, English
Religion: Roman Catholic 98%
Currency: Maltese Lira = 100 cents
Annual Income per person: $7,341
Annual Trade per person: $9,311
Adult Literacy: 85%
Life Expectancy (F): 76
Life Expectancy (M): 72

Location Map

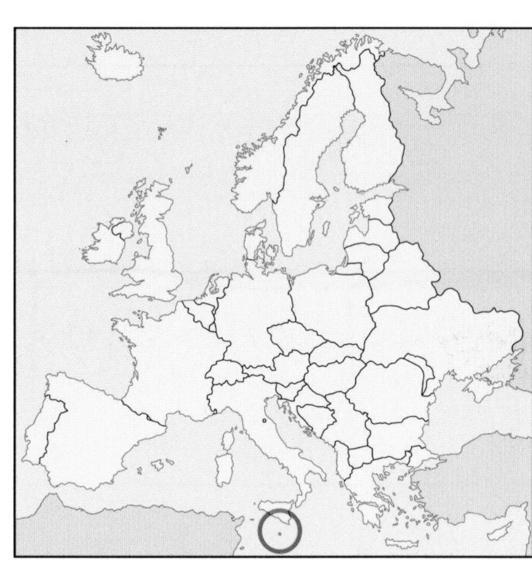

MOLDOVA

Facts and Figures

Capital: Chisinau 676,000 (1990)
Area (sq km): 33,700
Population: 4,400,000 (1992)
Language: Moldavian, Russian
Religion: Russian Orthodox, Evangelical
Currency: Leu
Annual Income per person: $2,170
Annual Trade per person: Data not available
Adult Literacy: Data not available
Life Expectancy (F): 72
Life Expectancy (M): 65

Location Map

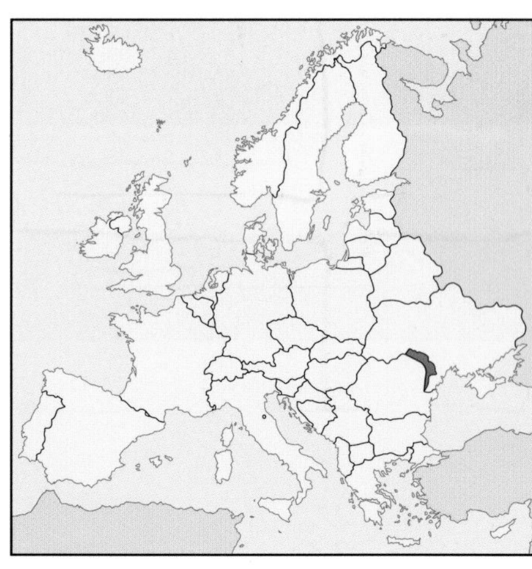

MONACO

Facts and Figures

Capital: Monaco 30,000 (1990)
Area (sq km): 1.5
Population: 30,000 (1990)
Language: French, Monégasque
Religion: Roman Catholic 95%
Currency: French
Annual Income per person: $16,000
Annual Trade per person: $30,000
Adult Literacy: 99%
Life Expectancy (F): 80
Life Expectancy (M): 72

Location Map

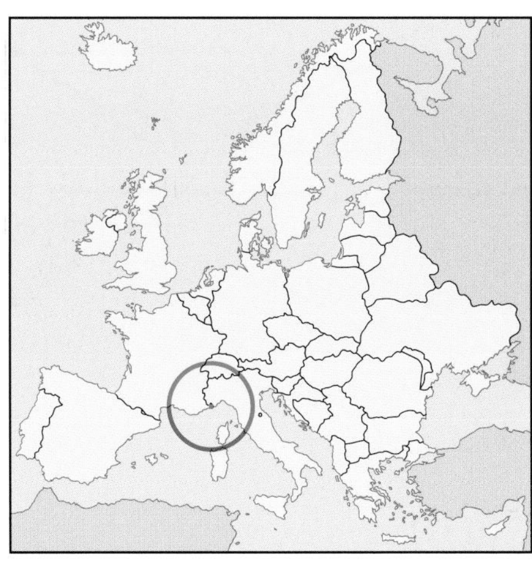

NETHERLANDS

Facts and Figures

Capital: Amsterdam 719,860 (1993)
Area (sq km): 41,530
Population: 15,240,000 (1993)
Language: Dutch
Religion: Roman Catholic 33% Protestant 23%
Currency: Guilder = 100 cents
Annual Income per person: $21,030
Annual Trade per person: $18,137
Adult Literacy: 99%
Life Expectancy (F): 81
Life Expectancy (M): 74

Location Map

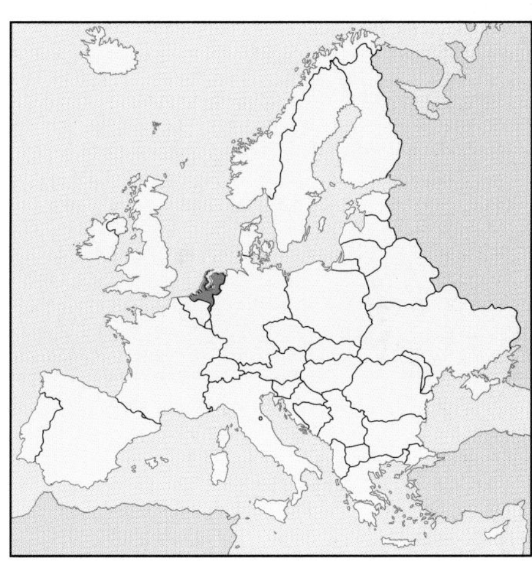

NORWAY

Facts and Figures

Capital: Oslo 473,350 (1992)
Area (sq km): 323,880
Population: 4,300,000 (1992)
Language: Norwegian, Lappish, Finnish
Religion: Lutheran 88% Roman Catholic
Currency: Norwegian Krone = 100 øre
Annual Income per person: $24,160
Annual Trade per person: $14,125
Adult Literacy: 99%
Life Expectancy (F): 81
Life Expectancy (M): 74

Location Map

Flags of Europe

POLAND

Facts and Figures

Capital: Warsaw 1,655,000 (1989)
Area (sq km): 312,680
Population: 38,310,000 (1993)
Language: Polish
Religion: Roman Catholic 94%
Currency: Zloty = 100 groszy
Annual Income per person: $1,830
Annual Trade per person: $751
Adult Literacy: 99%
Life Expectancy (F): 76
Life Expectancy (M): 67

Location Map

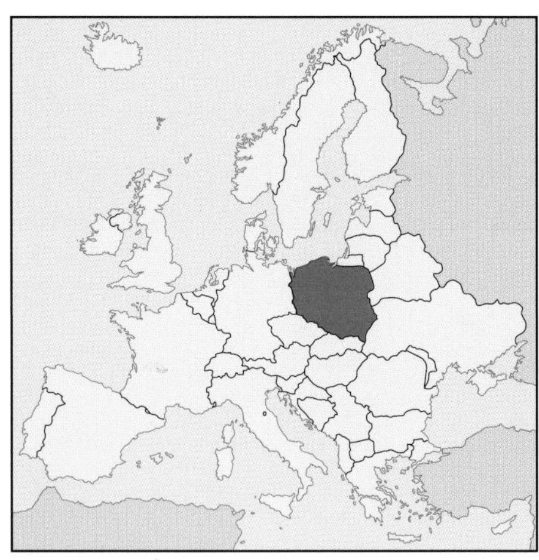

PORTUGAL

Facts and Figures

Capital: Lisbon 830,500 (1987)
Area (sq km): 91,900
Population: 9,860,000 (1991)
Language: Portuguese
Religion: Roman Catholic
Currency: Escudo = 100 centavos
Annual Income per person: $5,620
Annual Trade per person: $4,836
Adult Literacy: 98%
Life Expectancy (F): 78
Life Expectancy (M): 71

Location Map

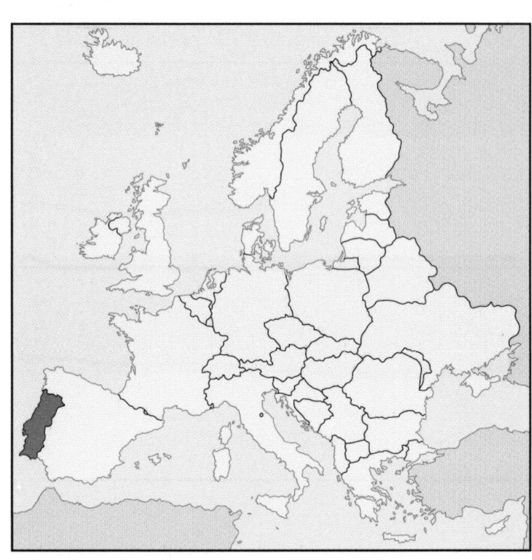

ROMANIA

Facts and Figures

Capital: Bucharest 2,351,000 (1992)
Area (sq km): 237,500
Population: 22,760,000 (1992)
Language: Romanian, Hungarian, German
Religion: Romanian Orthodox 87% RC 5%
Currency: Leu = 100 bani
Annual Income per person: $1,340
Annual Trade per person: $680
Adult Literacy: 96%
Life Expectancy (F): 74
Life Expectancy (M): 69

Location Map

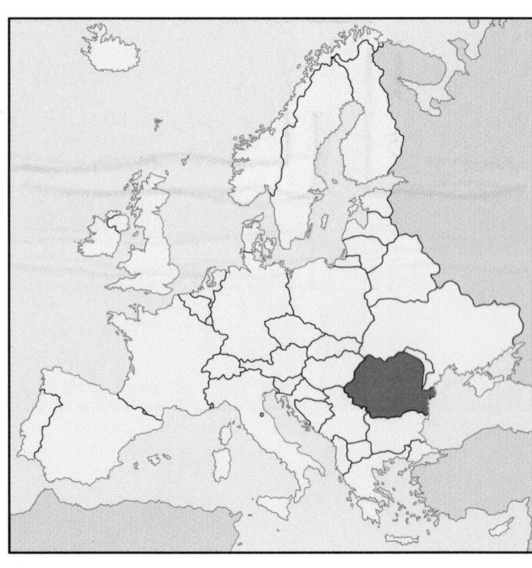

SAN MARINO

Facts and Figures

Capital: San Marino 4,335 (1993)
Area (sq km): 61
Population: 24,000 (1993)
Language: Italian
Religion: Roman Catholic
Currency: Italian Lira
Annual Income per person: $17,000
Annual Trade per person: $4,335
Adult Literacy: 96%
Life Expectancy (F): 79
Life Expectancy (M): 74

Location Map

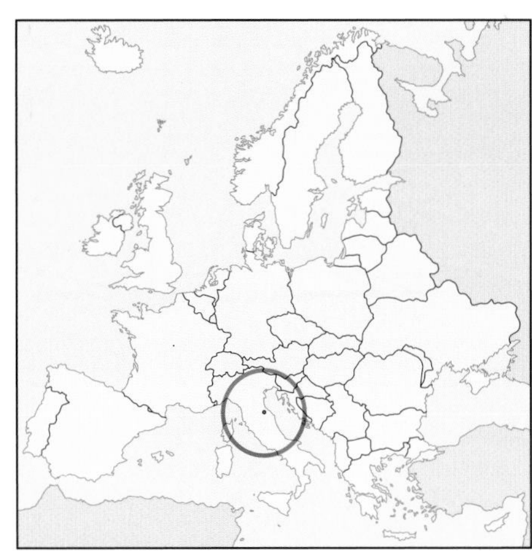

SLOVAKIA

Facts and Figures

Capital: Bratislava 440,421 (1990)
Area (sq km): 49,035
Population: 5,334,000 (1992)
Language: Slovak
Religion: Roman Catholic 22%
Currency: Slovak Koruna
Annual Income per person: No data available
Annual Trade per person: No data available
Adult Literacy: 99%
Life Expectancy (F): 76
Life Expectancy (M): 69

Location Map

SLOVENIA

Facts and Figures

Capital: Ljubljana 268,000 (1991)
Area (sq km): 20,251
Population: 2,000,000 (1992)
Language: Slovene, Serbo-Croat
Religion: Roman Catholic 94%
Currency: Slovene Tolar
Annual Income per person: $10,000
Annual Trade per person: $5,000
Adult Literacy: 99%
Life Expectancy (F): 75
Life Expectancy (M): 67

Location Map

Flags of Europe

SPAIN

Facts and Figures

Capital: Madrid 2,909,800 (1991)
Area (sq km): 504,750
Population: 39,080,000 (1992)
Language: Castilian Spanish, Basque, Catalan, Galician
Religion: Roman Catholic 97%
Currency: Peseta
Annual Income per person: $14,290
Annual Trade per person: $3,934
Adult Literacy: 96%
Life Expectancy (F): 80
Life Expectancy (M): 74

Location Map

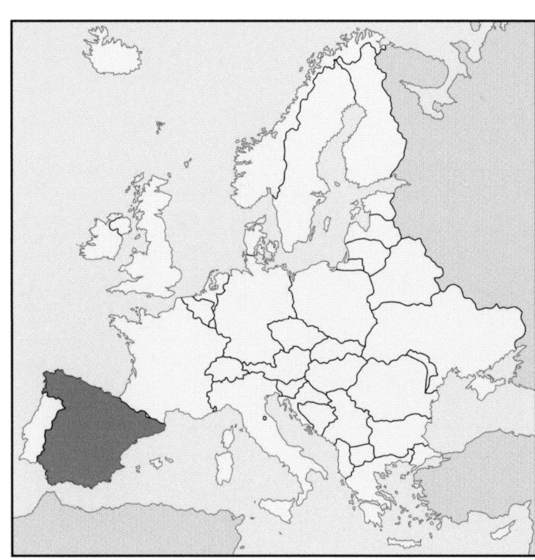

SWEDEN

Facts and Figures

Capital: Stockholm 684,580 (1992)
Area (sq km): 449,960
Population: 8,700,000 (1992)
Language: Swedish, Finnish
Religion: Lutheran 89%
Currency: Krona = 100 öre
Annual Income per person: $25,490
Annual Trade per person: $12,158
Adult Literacy: 99%
Life Expectancy (F): 81
Life Expectancy (M): 75

Location Map

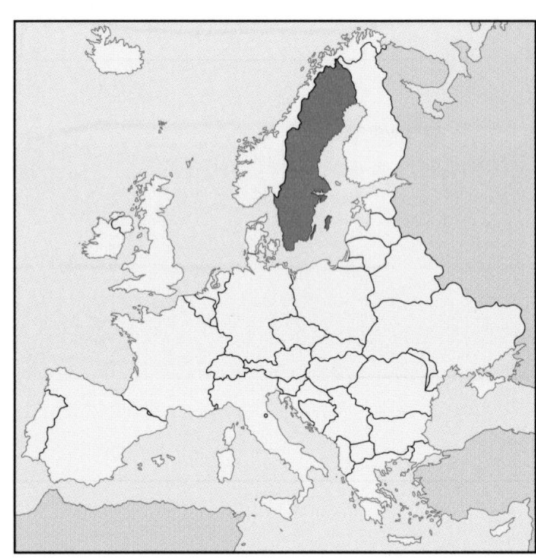

SWITZERLAND

Facts and Figures

Capital: Berne 298,700 (1990)
Area (sq km): 41,130
Population: 6,900,000 (1993)
Language: German, French, Italian, Romansch
Religion: Protestant 47% Roman Catholic 46%
Currency: Swiss Franc = 100 centimes
Annual Income per person: $32,250
Annual Trade per person: $19,088
Adult Literacy: 99%
Life Expectancy (F): 81
Life Expectancy (M): 75

Location Map

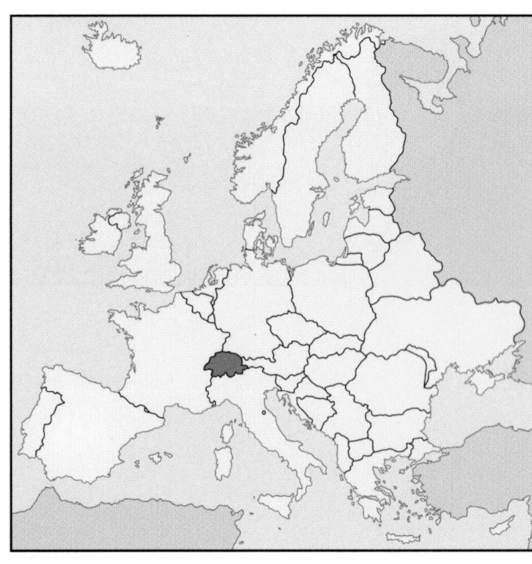

TURKEY

Facts and Figures

Capital: Ankara 3,022,000 (1990)
Area (sq km): 779,450
Population: 59,870,000 (1993)
Language: Turkish, Kurdish
Religion: Sunni Muslim 64% Shi'ite Muslim 28%
Currency: Turkish Lira = 100 kurus
Annual Income per person: $1,820
Annual Trade per person: $586
Adult Literacy: 81%
Life Expectancy (F): 68
Life Expectancy (M): 65

Location Map

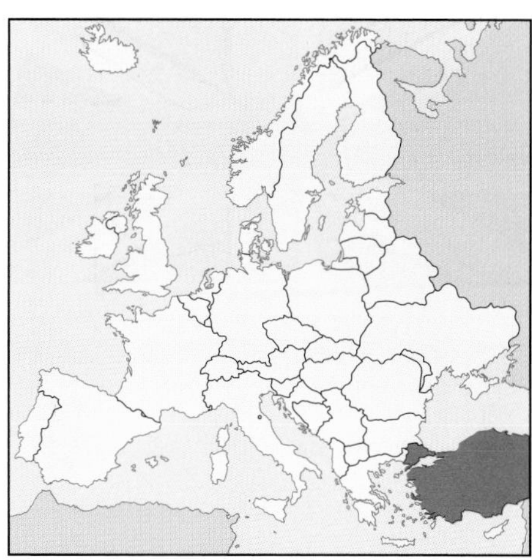

UKRAINE

Facts and Figures

Capital: Kiev 2,616,000 (1990)
Area (sq km): 603,700
Population: 52,100,000 (1992)
Language: Ukrainian, Russian
Religion: Ukrainian Orthodox, Roman Catholic
Currency: Rouble = 100 kopeks
Annual Income per person: $2,340
Annual Trade per person: $600
Adult Literacy: Data not available
Life Expectancy (F): 75
Life Expectancy (M): 66

Location Map

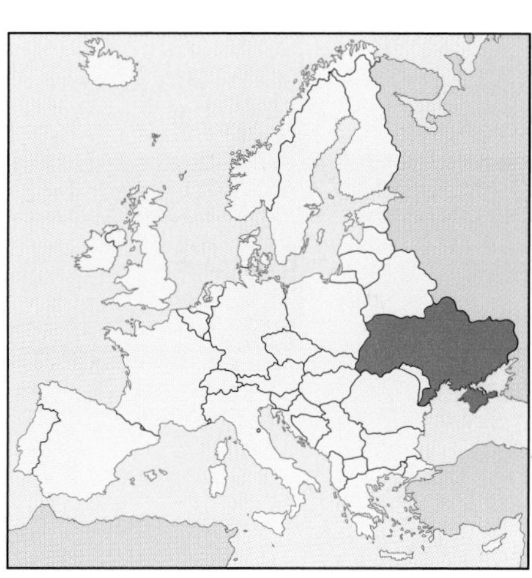

Flags of Europe

UNITED KINGDOM

Facts and Figures

Capital: London 6,679,700 (1991)
Area (sq km): 242,516
Population: 58,000,000
Language: English, Welsh, Scots-Gaelic
Religion: Anglican 57% Roman Catholic 13%
Currency: Pound Sterling =100 pence
Annual Income per person: $16,080
Annual Trade per person: $7,140
Adult Literacy: 99%
Life Expectancy (F): 79
Life Expectancy (M): 73

Location Map

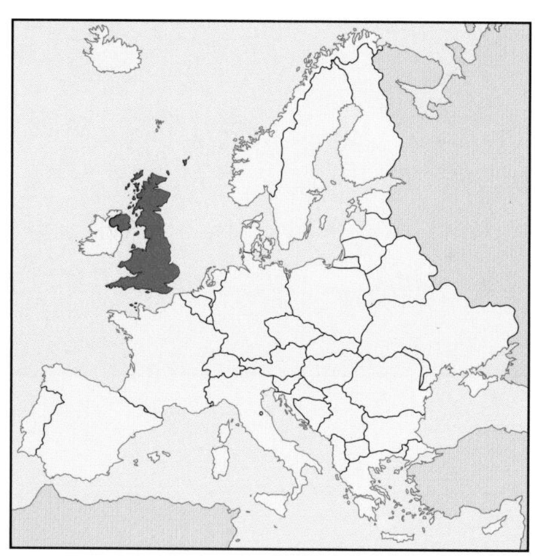

ENGLAND

Facts and Figures

Capital: London 6,679,700 (1991)
Area (sq km): 130,439
Population: 47,536,000
Language: English
Religion: Protestant, Roman Catholic, Judaism, Islam
Currency: Pound Sterling = 100 pence

Location Map

SCOTLAND

Facts and Figures

Capital: Edinburgh 433,000
Area (sq km): 78,772
Population: 5,094,000
Language: English
Religion: Protestant, Roman Catholic
Currency: Pound Sterling = 100 pence

Location Map

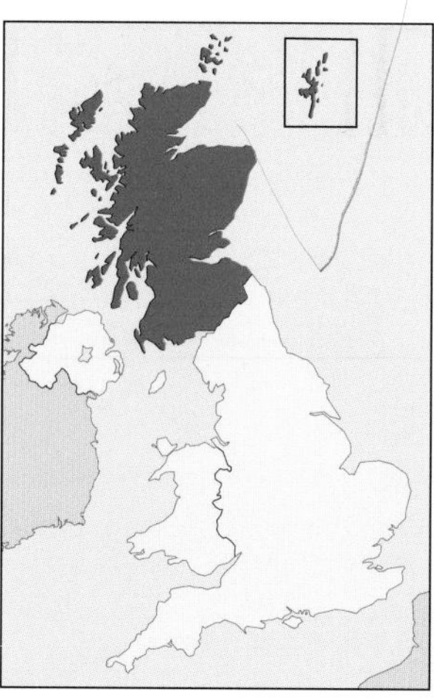

WALES

Facts and Figures

Capital: Cardiff 284,000
Area (sq km): 20,768
Population: 2,857,000
Language: English, Welsh
Religion: Protestant, Roman Catholic
Currency: Pound Sterling = 100 pence

Location Map

N. IRELAND

Facts and Figures

Capital: Belfast 300,000
Area (sq km): 14,121
Population: 1,578,000
Language: English
Religion: Protestant, Roman Catholic
Currency: Pound Sterling = 100 pence

Location Map

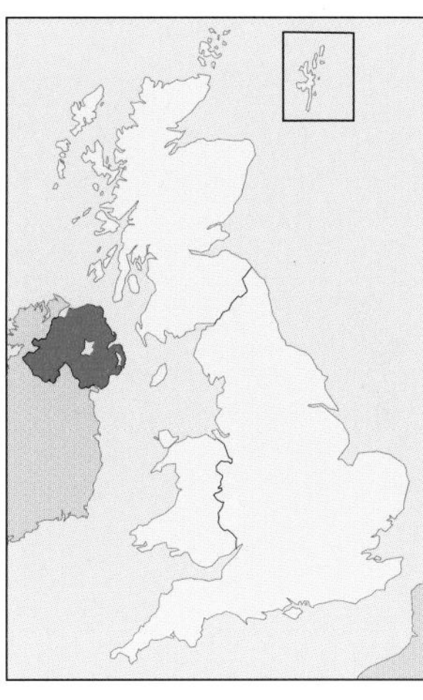

YUGOSLAVIA

Facts and Figures

Capital: Belgrade 1,168,000 (1991)
Area (sq km): 102,000
Population: 10,460,000(1992)
Language: Serbo-Croat
Religion: Orthodox 65%, Muslim 19%
Currency: Dinar = 100 paras
Annual Income per person: $4,500
Annual Trade per person: $1,000
Adult Literacy: 89%
Life Expectancy (F): 75
Life Expectancy (M): 69

Location Map

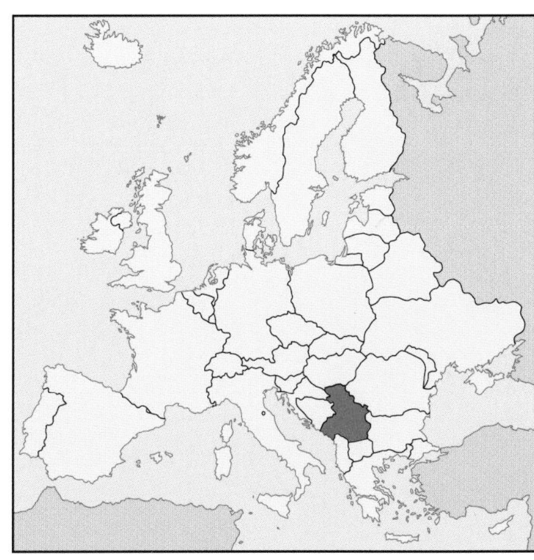

Flags of North & Central America

NORTH & CENTRAL AMERICA FLAG INDEX

Flags of North & Central America

ANTIGUA & BARBUDA

Facts and Figures

Capital: St. John's 30,000 (1982)
Area (sq km): 442
Population: 77,000 (1991)
Language: English
Religion: Protestant
Currency: Eastern Caribbean Dollar
Annual Income per person: $4,770
Annual Trade per person: Data not available
Adult Literacy: 96%
Life Expectancy (F): 74
Life Expectancy (M): 70

Location Map

BAHAMAS

Facts and Figures

Capital: Nassau 172,000 (1990)
Area (sq km): 13,864
Population: 264,000 (1992)
Language: English, Creole
Religion: Protestant 69% Roman Catholic 26%
Currency: Bahamian Dollar
Annual Income per person: $11,720
Annual Trade per person: $21,531
Adult Literacy: 99%
Life Expectancy (F): 76
Life Expectancy (M): 69

Location Map

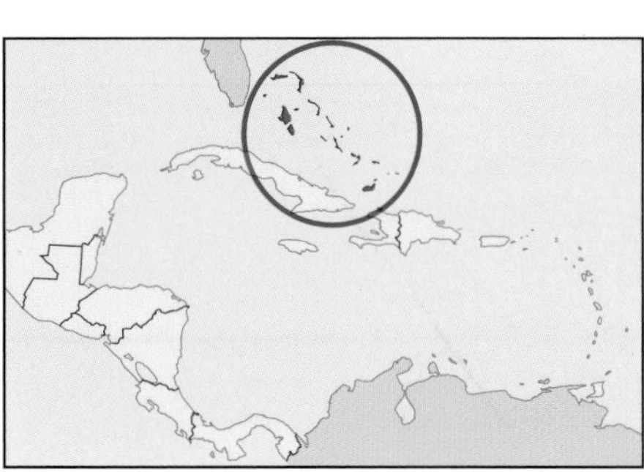

BARBADOS

Facts and Figures

Capital: Bridgetown 6,720 (1990)
Area (sq km): 430
Population: 258,600 (1991)
Language: English, Creole
Religion: Protestant 56% Roman Catholic 4%
Currency: Barbados Dollar
Annual Income per person: $6,630
Annual Trade per person: $3,450
Adult Literacy: 99%
Life Expectancy (F): 78
Life Expectancy (M): 73

Location Map

Flags of North & Central America

BERMUDA

Facts and Figures

Capital: Hamilton 3,440 (1990)
Area (sq km): 53
Population: 71,950 (1992)
Language: English
Religion: Protestant 62% Roman Catholic 14%
Currency: Bermuda Dollar
Annual Income per person: $24,000
Annual Trade per person: $9,750
Adult Literacy: 98%
Life Expectancy (F): 78
Life Expectancy (M): 72

Location Map

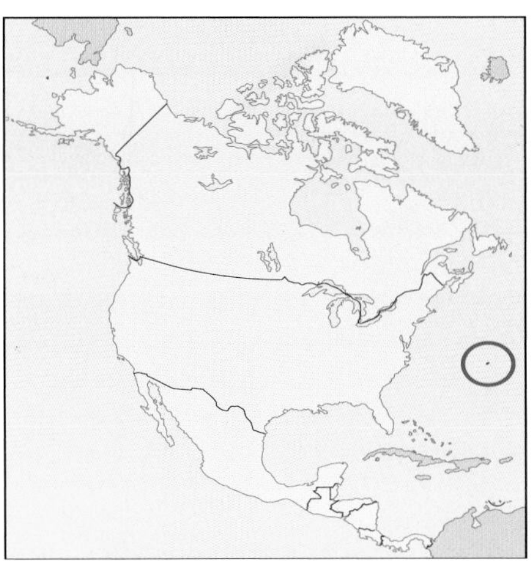

BELIZE

Facts and Figures

Capital: Belmopan 5,276 (1990)
Area (sq km): 22,960
Population: 230,000 (1993)
Language: English, Creole, Spanish
Religion: Roman Catholic 62% Protestant 28%
Currency: Belize Dollar
Annual Income per person: $2,050
Annual Trade per person: $1,953
Adult Literacy: 95%
Life Expectancy (F): 72
Life Expectancy (M): 67

Location Map

CANADA

Facts and Figures

Capital: Ottawa 314,000 (1991)
Area (sq km): 9,970,610
Population: 27,400,000 (1992)
Language: English, French
Religion: Roman Catholic 47% Protestant 41%
Currency: Canadian Dollar
Annual Income per person: $21,260
Annual Trade per person: $9,355
Adult Literacy: 99%
Life Expectancy (F): 81
Life Expectancy (M): 74

Location Map

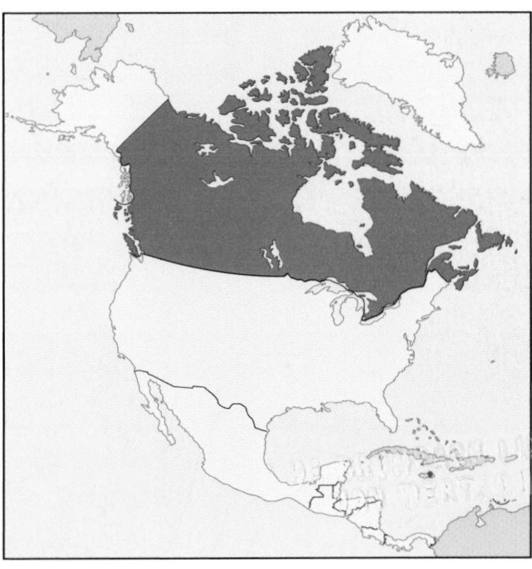

Flags of North & Central America

COSTA RICA

Facts and Figures

Capital: San José 245,000 (1984)
Area (sq km): 51,100
Population: 3,300,000 (1991)
Language: Spanish,Creole
Religion: Roman Catholic 90%
Currency: Colon=100 céntimos
Annual Income per person: $1,930
Annual Trade per person: $1,110
Adult Literacy: 93%
Life Expectancy (F): 78
Life Expectancy (M): 73

Location Map

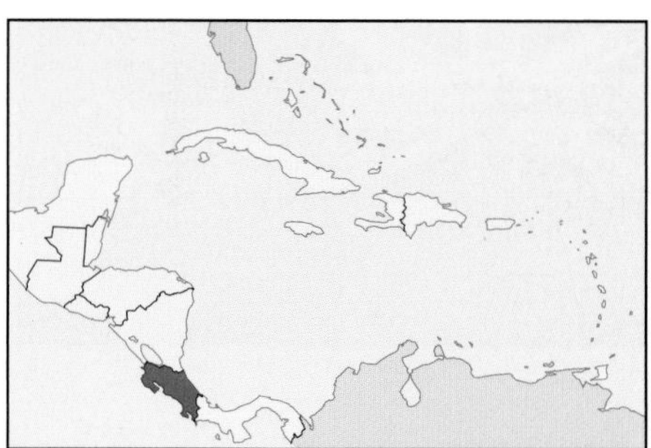

CUBA

Facts and Figures

Capital: Havana 2,014,800 (1986)
Area (sq km): 110,860
Population: 10,700,000 (1991)
Language: Spanish
Religion: Roman Catholic 39% Protestant 3%
Currency: Cuban peso =100centavos
Annual Income per person: $1,000
Annual Trade per person: $678
Adult Literacy: 75%
Life Expectancy (F): 78
Life Expectancy (M): 74

Location Map

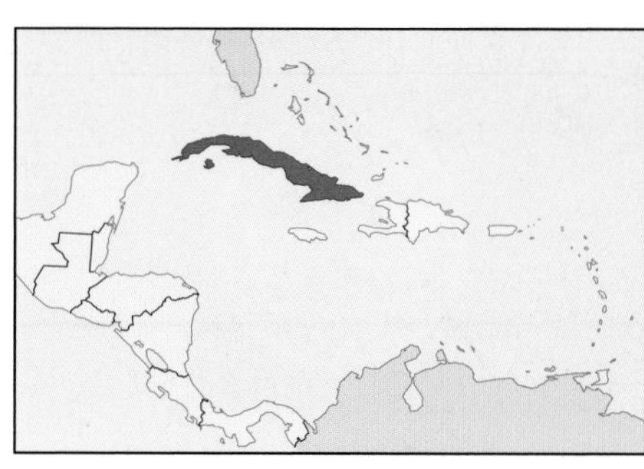

DOMINICA

Facts and Figures

Capital: Roseau 20,000 (1991)
Area (sq km): 751
Population: 108,800 (1991)
Language: English, French patois
Religion: Roman Catholic 80% Protestant 15%
Currency: East Caribbean Dollar=100cents
Annual Income per person: $2,440
Annual Trade per person: $2,163
Adult Literacy: 97%
Life Expectancy (F): 79
Life Expectancy (M): 73

Location Map

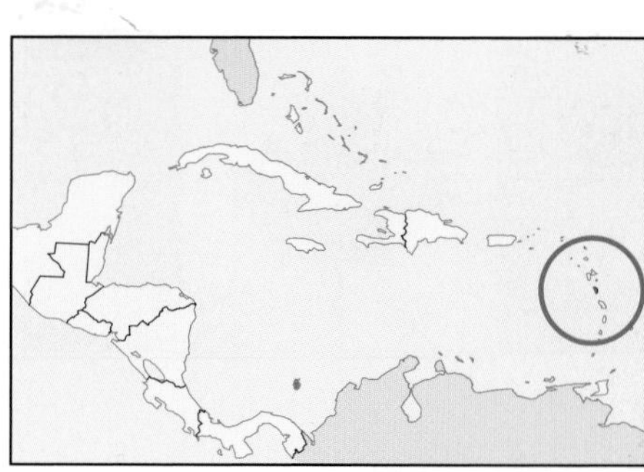

DOMINICAN REPUBLIC

Facts and Figures

Capital: Santo Domingo 1,601,000 (1986)
Area (sq km): 48,442
Population: 7,310,000 (1991)
Language: Spanish
Religion: Roman Catholic 92%
Currency: Peso = 100centavos
Annual Income per person: $950
Annual Trade per person: $324
Adult Literacy: 83%
Life Expectancy (F): 70
Life Expectancy (M): 65

Location Map

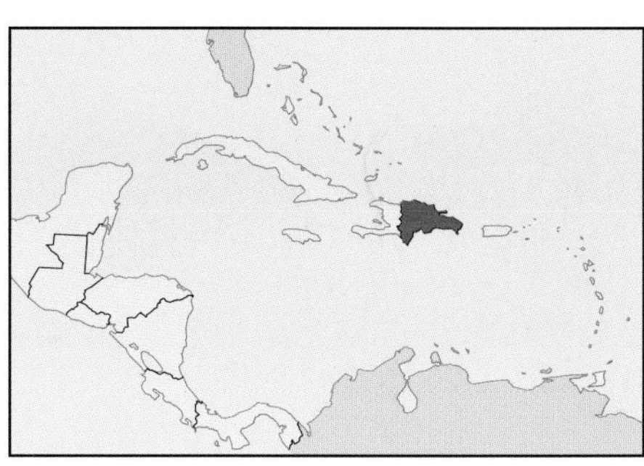

EL SALVADOR

Facts and Figures

Capital: San Salvador 1,522,130 (1992)
Area (sq km): 21,041
Population: 5,050,000 (1992)
Language: Spanish
Religion: Roman Catholic 91% Protestant 4%
Currency: Colón= 100centavos
Annual Income per person: $1,070
Annual Trade per person: $250
Adult Literacy: 73%
Life Expectancy (F): 69
Life Expectancy (M): 64

Location Map

GREENLAND

Facts and Figures

Capital: Godthåb (Nuuk) 12,200 (1993)
Area (sq km): 2,175,600
Population: 55,000 (1993)
Language: Eskimo dialects, Danish
Religion: Evanjelical Lutherans 98%
Currency: Danish Krone = 100 ore
Annual Income per person: $6,000
Annual Trade per person: $15,017
Adult Literacy: Data not available
Life Expectancy (F): 69
Life Expectancy (M): 63

Location Map

Flags of North & Central America

GRENADA

Facts and Figures

Capital: St George's 35,750 (1980)
Area (sq km): 344
Population: 95,350 (1993)
Language: English, French patois
Religion: Roman Catholic 53% Anglican 14% Seventh Day Adventist 9% Pentecostal 7%
Currency: Eastern Caribbean $
Annual Income per person: $2,180
Annual Trade per person: $1,342
Adult Literacy: 96%
Life Expectancy (F): 74
Life Expectancy (M): 69

Location Map

GUATEMALA

Facts and Figures

Capital: Guatemala City 2,000,000 (1989)
Area (sq km): 108,890
Population: 9,740,000 (1992)
Language: Spanish, Indian dialects
Religion: Roman Catholic 71% Pentecostal 23% Other Protestant 7%
Currency: Quetzal = 100 centavos
Annual Income per person: $930
Annual Trade per person: $286
Adult Literacy: 55%
Life Expectancy (F): 67
Life Expectancy (M): 62

Location Map

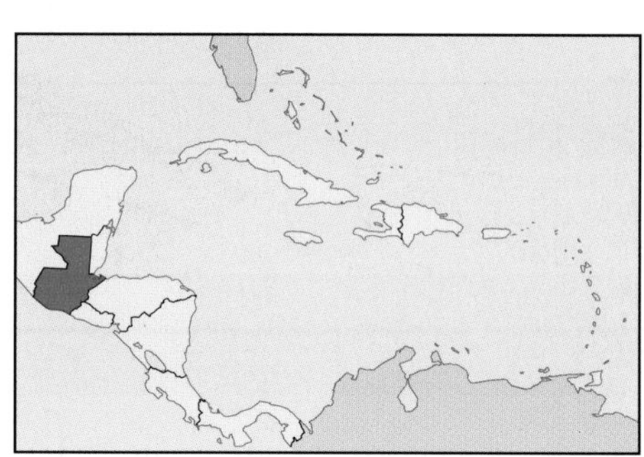

HAITI

Facts and Figures

Capital: Port-au-Prince 1,402,000 (1991)
Area (sq km): 27,750
Population: 6,760,000 (1992)
Language: Haitian Créole,French
Religion: Roman Catholic 75% Other Christian 10% Voodoo
Currency: Gourde = 100 centimes
Annual Income per person: $370
Annual Trade per person: $70
Adult Literacy: 53%
Life Expectancy (F): 58
Life Expectancy (M): 55

Location Map

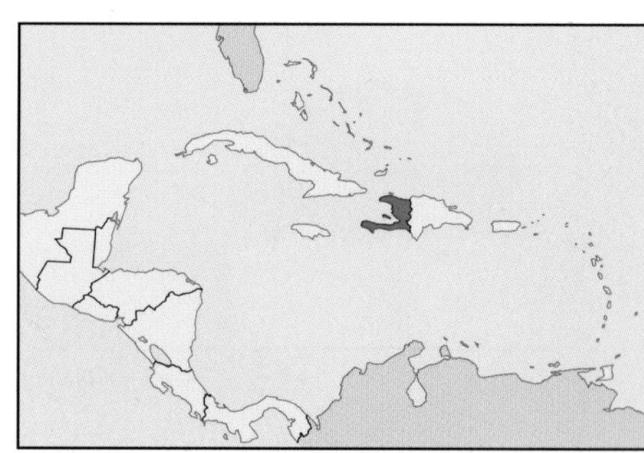

Flags of North & Central America

HONDURAS

Facts and Figures

Capital: Tegucigalpa 678,700 (1988)
Area (sq km): 112,088
Population: 5,260,000
Language: Spanish
Religion: Roman Catholic 97%
Currency: Lempira = 100 centavos
Annual Income per person: $570
Annual Trade per person: $321
Adult Literacy: 73%
Life Expectancy (F): 68
Life Expectancy (M): 64

Location Map

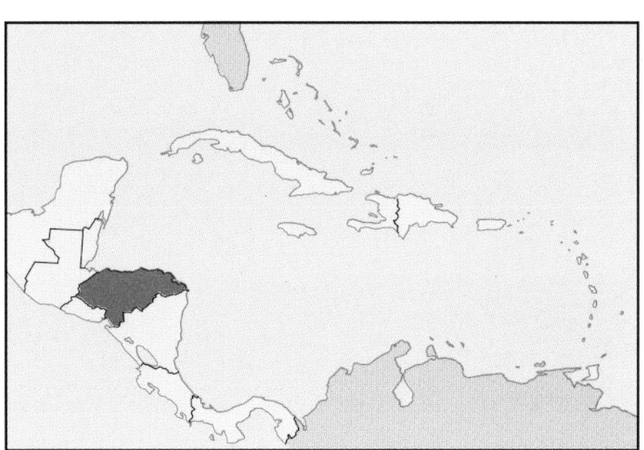

JAMAICA

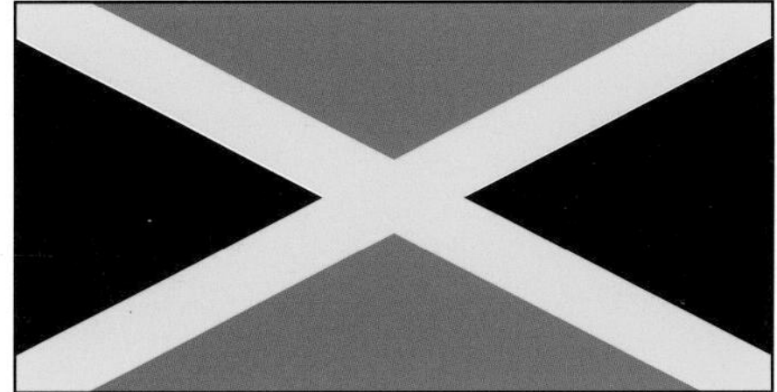

Facts and Figures

Capital: Kingston 587.800 (1991)
Area (sq km): 11,425
Population: 2,450,000 (1992)
Language: English, English Creole
Religion: Protestant 70% Roman Catholic 8%
Currency: Jamaican Dollar $
Annual Income per person: $1,380
Annual Trade per person: $1,242
Adult Literacy: 98%
Life Expectancy (F): 76
Life Expectancy (M): 71

Location Map

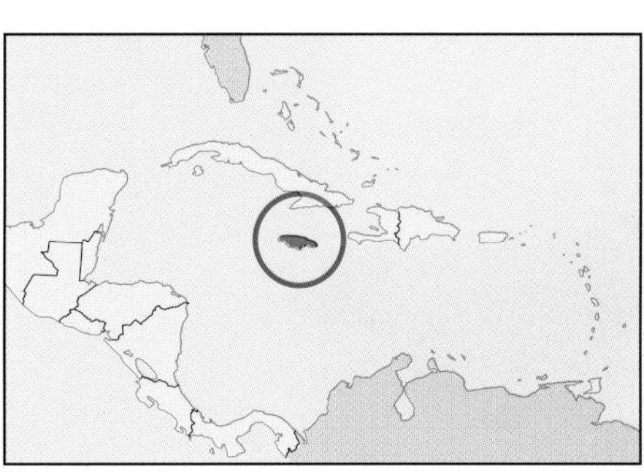

MEXICO

Facts and Figures

Capital: Mexico City 15,047,770 (1990)
Area (sq km): 1,967,200
Population: 91,600,000 (1992)
Language: Spanish
Religion: Roman Catholic 94% Protestant 3%
Currency: Peso = 100 centavos
Annual Income per person: $2,870
Annual Trade per person: $743
Adult Literacy: 87%
Life Expectancy (F): 74
Life Expectancy (M): 67

Location Map

Flags of North & Central America

NICARAGUA

Facts and Figures

Capital: Managua 682,100 (1985)
Area (sq km): 130,682
Population: 4,200,000 (1991)
Language: Spanish
Religion: Roman Catholic 88%
Currency: Córdoba =100centavos
Annual Income per person: $340
Annual Trade per person: $349
Adult Literacy: 81%
Life Expectancy (F): 68
Life Expectancy (M): 65

Location Map

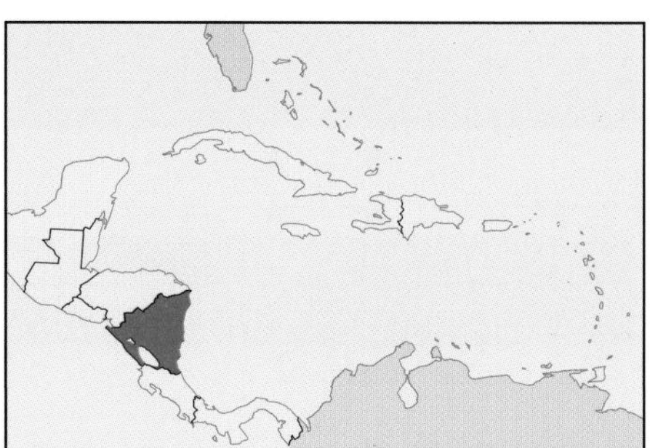

PANAMA

Facts and Figures

Capital: Panama City 584,800 (1990)
Area (sq km): 77,080
Population: 2,330,000 (1990)
Language: Spanish, English
Religion: Roman Catholic 85%
Protestant 5% Moslem 5%
Currency: Balboa = 100centesimos
Annual Income per person: $2180
Annual Trade per person: $825
Adult Literacy: 72%
Life Expectancy (F): 75
Life Expectancy (M): 71

Location Map

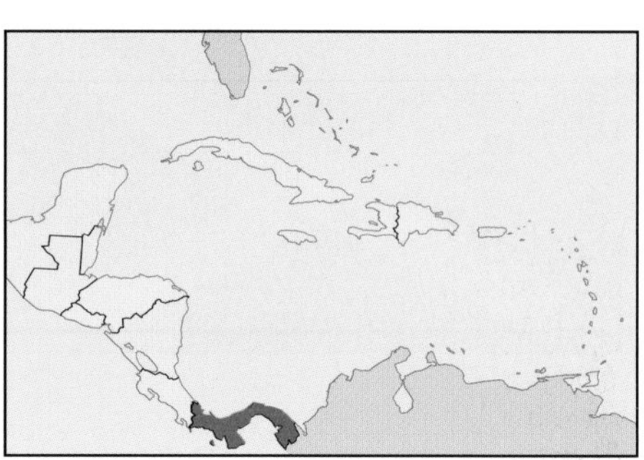

ST. CHRISTOPHER NEVIS

Facts and Figures

Capital: Basseterre 14,300 (1980)
Area (sq km): 262
Population: 40,620 (1991)
Language: English
Religion: Protestant 76% Roman Catholic 11%
Currency: East Caribbean Dollar=100cents
Annual Income per person: $3,960
Annual Trade per person: $3,200
Adult Literacy: 92%
Life Expectancy (F): 71
Life Expectancy (M): 64

Location Map

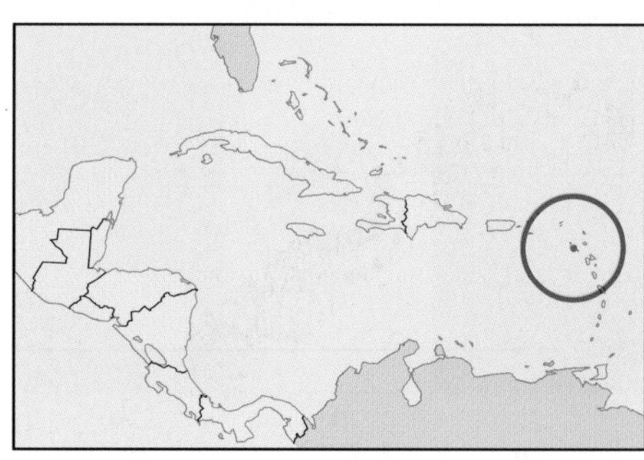

ST. LUCIA

Facts and Figures

Capital: Castries 53,900 (1992)
Area (sq km): 617
Population: 136,000 (1992)
Language: English,French patois
Religion: Roman Catholic 82% Protestant 10%
Currency: East Caribbean Dollar=100cents
Annual Income per person: $2,500
Annual Trade per person: $2,267
Adult Literacy: 93%
Life Expectancy (F): 74
Life Expectancy (M): 69

Location Map

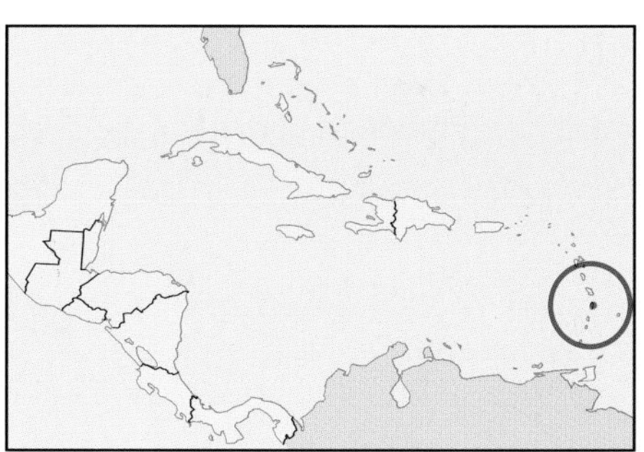

ST. VINCENT

Facts and Figures

Capital: Kingstown 26,600 (1991)
Area (sq km): 388
Population: 107,600 (1991)
Language: English,French patois
Religion: Protestant 53% Roman Catholic 12%
Currency: East Caribbean Dollar=100cents
Annual Income per person: $1,730
Annual Trade per person: $1,800
Adult Literacy: 84%
Life Expectancy (F): 72
Life Expectancy (M): 68

Location Map

TRINIDAD & TOBAGO

Facts and Figures

Capital: Port-of-Spain 58,400 (1990)
Area (sq km): 5,124
Population: 1,250,000 (1991)
Language: English
Religion: Roman Catholic 29% Protestant 11%
Hindu 24% Muslim 6%
Currency: Trinidad and Tobago $ =100cents
Annual Income per person: $3,620
Annual Trade per person: $2,902
Adult Literacy: 96%
Life Expectancy (F): 75
Life Expectancy (M): 70

Location Map

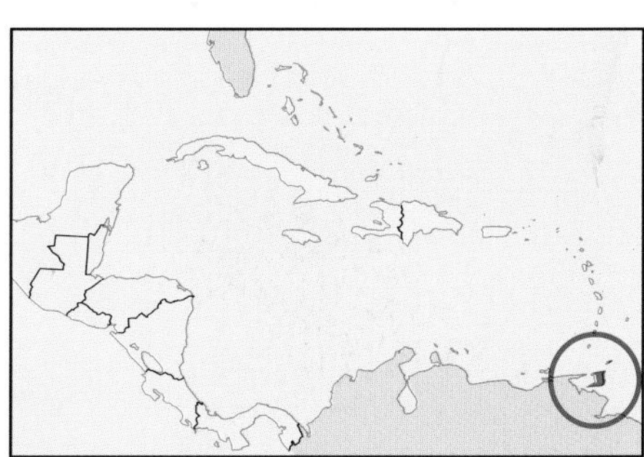

Flags of The United States of America

Flags of The United States of America

U.S.A FLAG INDEX

Flags of The United States of America

USA

Facts and Figures

Capital: Washington D. C. 606,900 (1990)
Area (sq km): 9,158,960
Population: 252,180,000 (1991)
Language: English, Spanish
Religion: Christian, Jewish
Currency: US Dollar = 100 cents
Annual Income per person: $22,560
Annual Trade per person: $3,922
Adult Literacy: 99%
Life Expectancy (F): 79
Life Expectancy (M): 72

Location Map

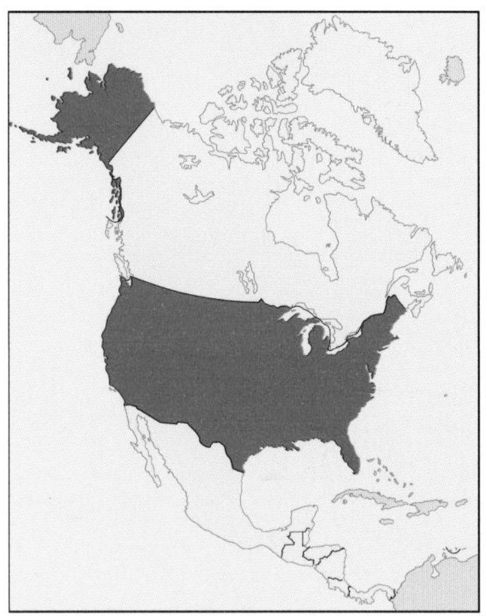

ALABAMA

ALASKA

ARIZONA

ARKANSAS

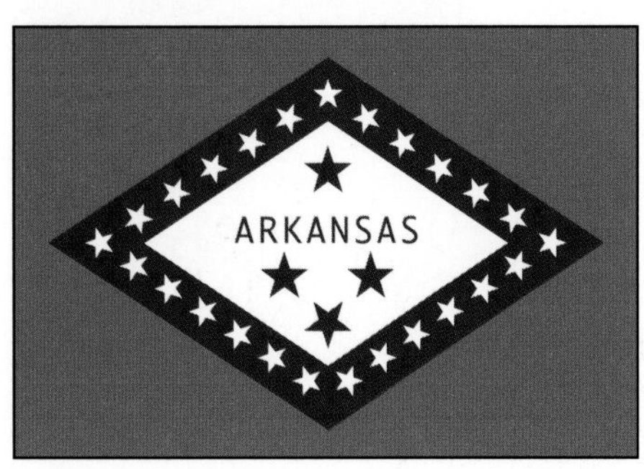

CALIFORNIA

COLORADO

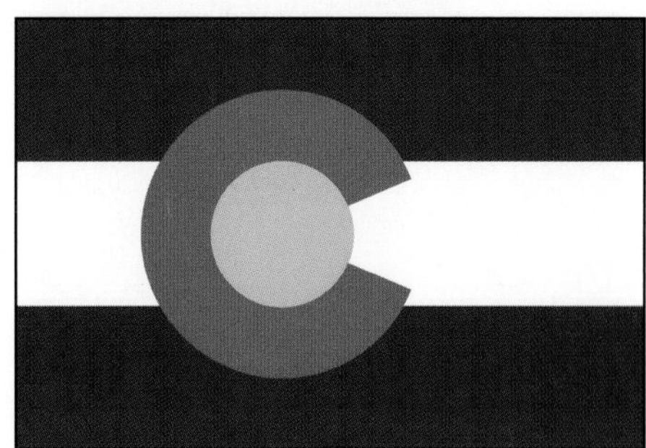

Flags of The United States of America

CONNECTICUT

DELAWARE

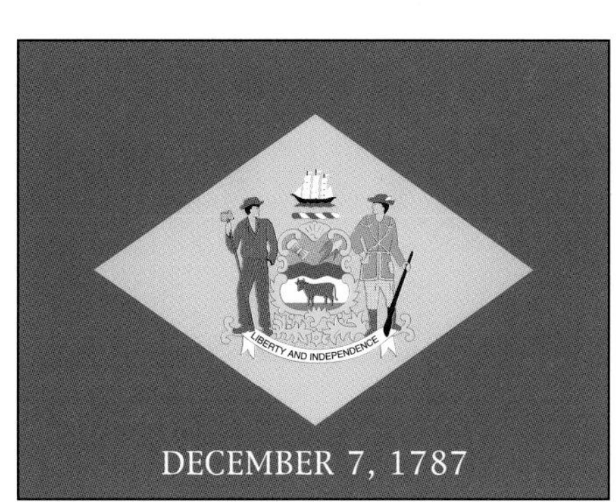

FLORIDA

GEORGIA

HAWAII

IDAHO

ILLINOIS

INDIANA

IOWA

Flags of The United States of America

KANSAS

KENTUCKY

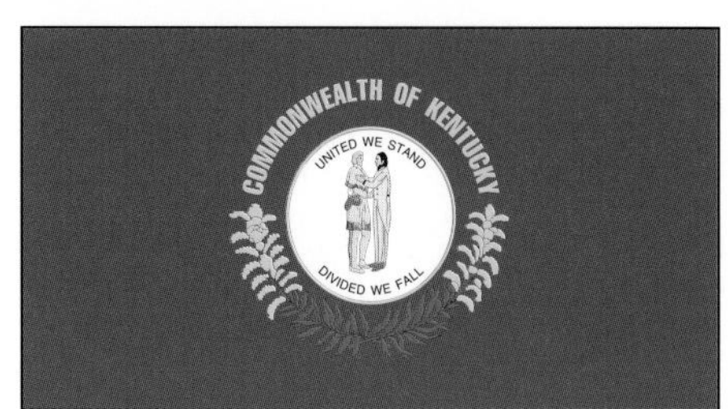

LOUISIANA

MAINE

MARYLAND

MASSACHUSETTS

MICHIGAN

MINNESOTA

MISSISSIPPI

Flags of The United States of America

MISSOURI

MONTANA

NEBRASKA

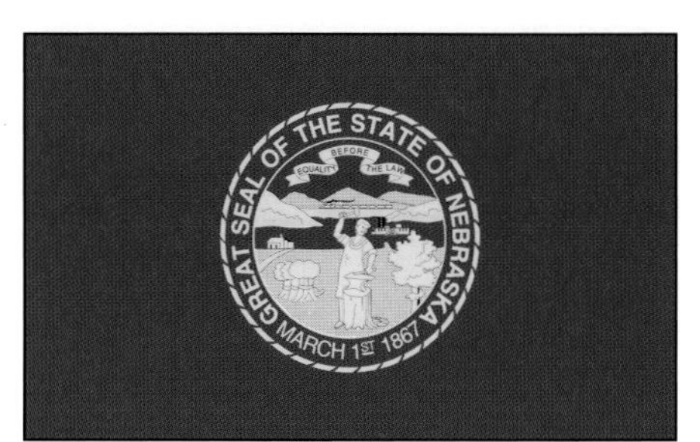

NEVADA

NEW HAMPSHIRE

NEW JERSEY

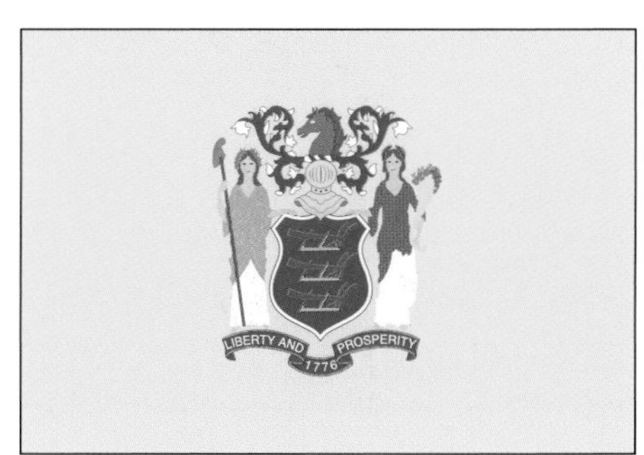

NEW MEXICO

NEW YORK

NORTH CAROLINA

Flags of The United States of America

NORTH DAKOTA

OHIO

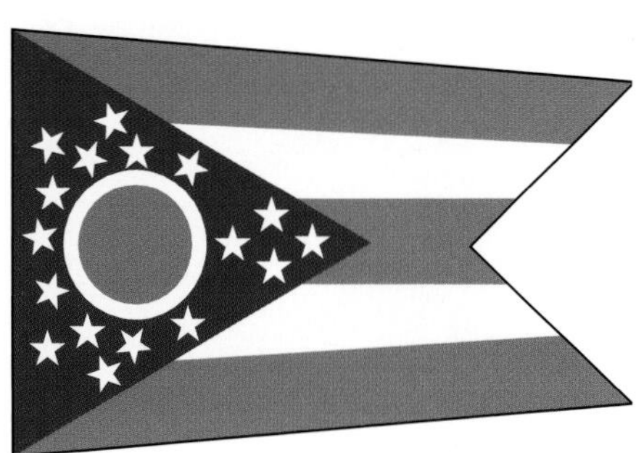

OKLAHOMA

OREGON

PENNSYLVANIA

RHODE ISLAND

SOUTH CAROLINA

SOUTH DAKOTA

TENNESSEE

Flags of The United States of America

TEXAS

UTAH

VERMONT

VIRGINIA

WASHINGTON

WEST VIRGINIA

WISCONSIN

WYOMING

Flags of South America

Flags of South America

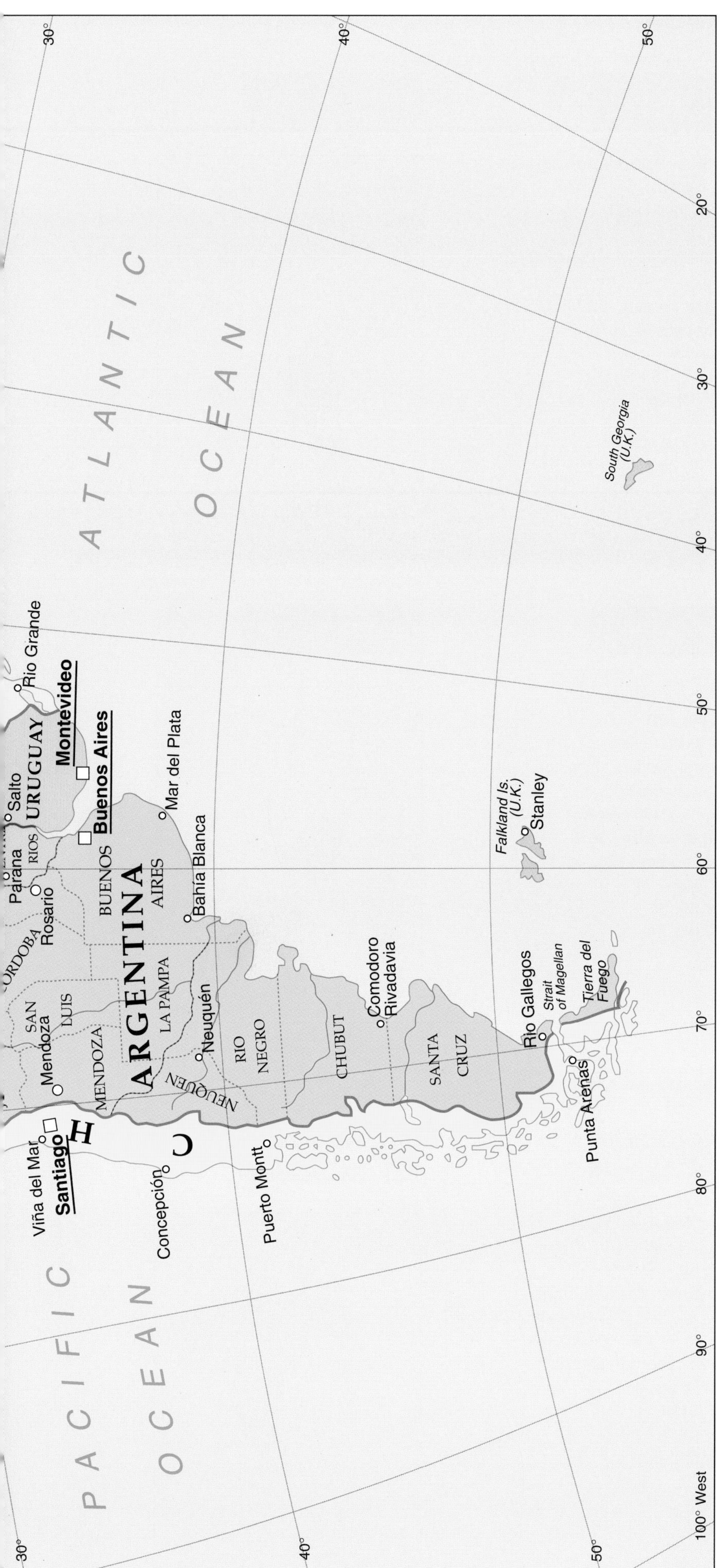

SOUTH AMERICA FLAG INDEX

Flags of South America

ARGENTINA

Facts and Figures

Capital: Buenos Aires 9,927,400 (1980)
Area (sq km): 2,780,092
Population: 32,370,000 (1991)
Language: Spanish
Religion: Roman Catholic 94% Protestant 2%
Currency: Peso
Annual Income per person: $2,780
Annual Trade per person: $613
Adult Literacy: 95%
Life Expectancy (F): 75
Life Expectancy (M): 68

Location Map

BOLIVIA

Facts and Figures

Capital: Sucre 105,800 (1988)
Area (sq km): 1,098,580
Population: 7,610,000 (1991)
Language: Spanish, Aymara, Quechua
Religion: Roman Catholic 89%
Currency: Boliviano = 100 centavos
Annual Income per person: $650
Annual Trade per person: $237
Adult Literacy: 78%
Life Expectancy (F): 58
Life Expectancy (M): 54

Location Map

BRAZIL

Facts and Figures

Capital: Brasilia 1,596,270 (1991)
Area (sq km): 8,511,996
Population: 159,100,000 (1991)
Language: Portuguese, Spanish, English
Religion: Roman Catholic 89% Protestant 7%
Currency: Cruzeiro Real = 100 centavos
Annual Income per person: $2,920
Annual Trade per person: $343
Adult Literacy: 81%
Life Expectancy (F): 69
Life Expectancy (M): 64

Location Map

Flags of South America

CHILE

Facts and Figures

Capital: Santiago 4,858,350 (1987)
Area (sq km): 736,900
Population: 13,440,000 (1993)
Language: Spanish
Religion: Roman Catholic 80% Protestant 6%
Currency: Chilean Peso = 100 centavos
Annual Income per person: $2,160
Annual Trade per person: $1,221
Adult Literacy: 93%
Life Expectancy (F): 76
Life Expectancy (M): 69

Location Map

COLOMBIA

Facts and Figures

Capital: Bogotá 4,921,300 (1992)
Area (sq km): 1,141,750
Population: 33,390,000 (1992)
Language: Spanish
Religion: Roman Catholic 94%
Currency: Colombian Peso = 100 centavos
Annual Income per person: $1,280
Annual Trade per person: $364
Adult Literacy: 87%
Life Expectancy (F): 72
Life Expectancy (M): 66

Location Map

ECUADOR

Facts and Figures

Capital: Quito 1,100,850 (1990)
Area (sq km): 272,045
Population: 9,650,000 (1990)
Language: Spanish, Quechua
Religion: Roman Catholic 91% Protestant 6%
Currency: Sucre = 100 centavos
Annual Income per person: $1,020
Annual Trade per person: $474
Adult Literacy: 86%
Life Expectancy (F): 69
Life Expectancy (M): 65

Location Map

Flags of South America

GUYANA

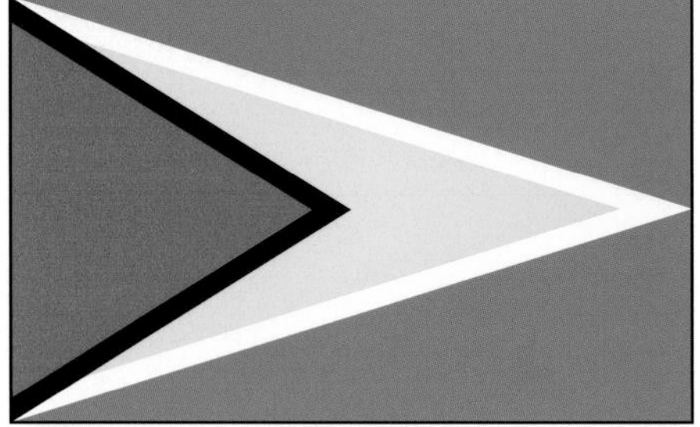

Facts and Figures

Capital: Georgetown 188,000 (1983)
Area (sq km): 214,970
Population: 990,000 (1989)
Language: English, Hindi, Urdu
Religion: Protestant 34% Hindu 34%
Roman Catholic 18% Muslim 9%
Currency: Guyanan Dollar = 100 cents
Annual Income per person: $290
Annual Trade per person: $959
Adult Literacy: 96%
Life Expectancy (F): 68
Life Expectancy (M): 62

Location Map

PARAGUAY

Facts and Figures

Capital: Asunción 607,700 (1990)
Area (sq km): 406,750
Population: 4,500,000 (1993)
Language: Spanish, Guaraní
Religion: Roman Catholic 96%
Currency: Guaraní = 100 céntimos
Annual Income per person: $1,210
Annual Trade per person: $447
Adult Literacy: 90%
Life Expectancy (F): 70
Life Expectancy (M): 65

Location Map

PERU

Facts and Figures

Capital: Lima 5,759,700 (1993)
Area (sq km): 1,244,300
Population: 22,130,000 (1993)
Language: Spanish, Quechua, Aymara
Religion: Roman Catholic 93%
Currency: Nuevo sol = 100centavos
Annual Income per person: $1,020
Annual Trade per person: $288
Adult Literacy: 85%
Life Expectancy (F): 67
Life Expectancy (M): 63

Location Map

SURINAM

Facts and Figures

Capital: Paramaribo 201,000 (1993)
Area (sq km): 163,820
Population: 404,310 (1991)
Language: Dutch, Spanish, English
Religion: Hindu 24% Roman Catholic 20%
Muslim 17% Protestant 16%
Other 7%
Currency: Surinam Guilder = 100cents
Annual Income per person: $3,610
Annual Trade per person: $2,100
Adult Literacy: 95%
Life Expectancy (F): 73
Life Expectancy (M): 68

Location Map

URUGUAY

Facts and Figures

Capital: Montevideo 1,383,700 (1992)
Area (sq km): 176,215
Population: 3,120,000 (1992)
Language: Spanish
Religion: Roman Catholic 56%
Currency: Uruguayan peso = 100 centésimos
Annual Income per person: $2,860
Annual Trade per person: $1,032
Adult Literacy: 96%
Life Expectancy (F): 76
Life Expectancy (M): 69

Location Map

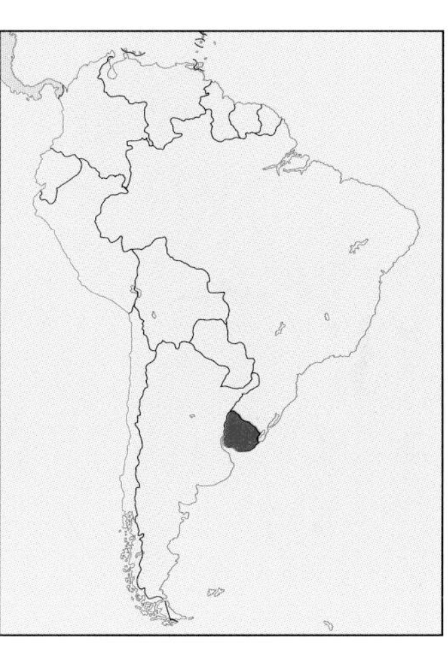

VENEZUELA

Facts and Figures

Capital: Caracas 1,044,900 (1981)
Area (sq km): 912,050
Population: 20,410,000 (1993)
Language: Spanish
Religion: Roman Catholic 86%
Currency: Bolívar =100 céntimos
Annual Income per person: $2,610
Annual Trade per person: $1,288
Adult Literacy: 88%
Life Expectancy (F): 74
Life Expectancy (M): 67

Location Map

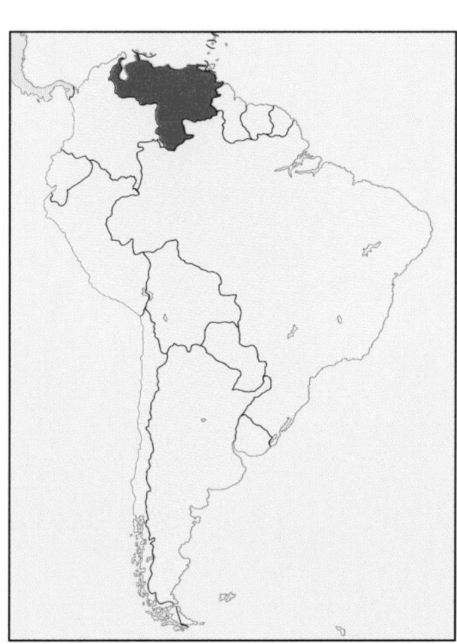

Flags of Africa

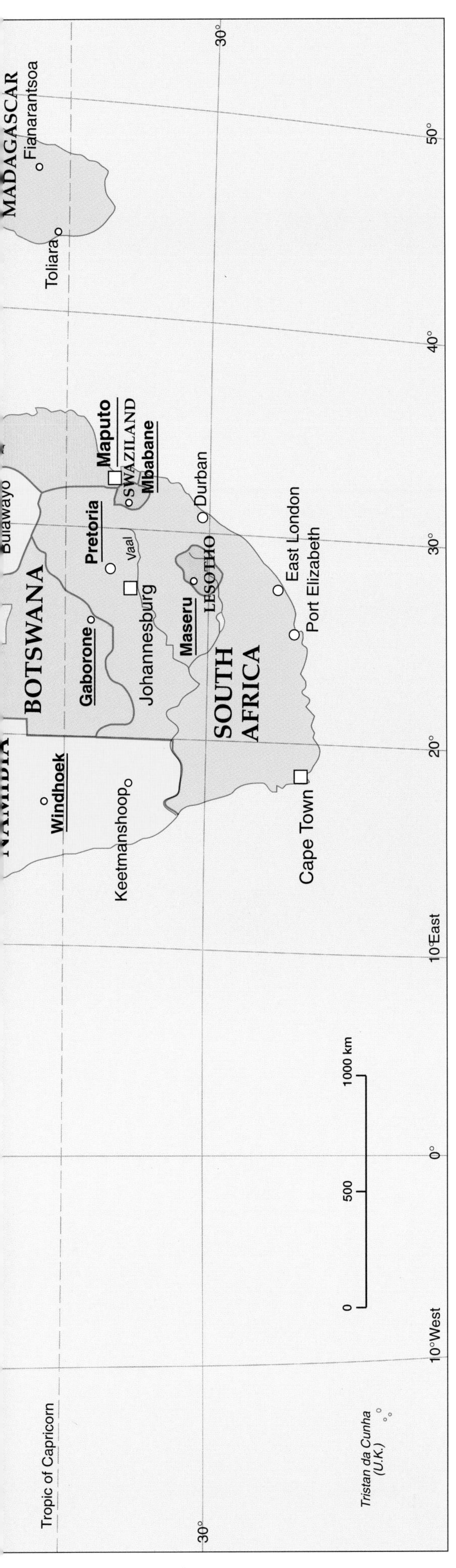

AFRICA FLAG INDEX

Flags of Africa

ALGERIA

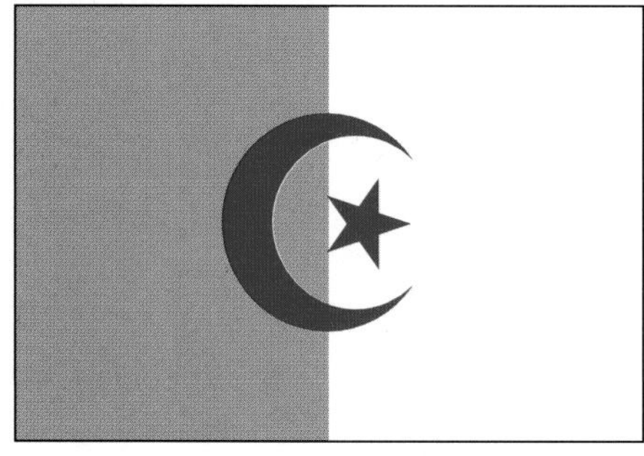

Facts and Figures

Capital: Algiers 1,507,000 (1987)
Area (sq km): 2,381,741
Population: 26,600,000 (1993)
Language: Arabic, French, Berber
Religion: Sunni Muslim 98%
Currency: Algerian Dinar = 100 centimes
Annual Income per person: $2,020
Annual Trade per person: $639
Adult Literacy: 57%
Life Expectancy (F): 67
Life Expectancy (M): 65

Location Map

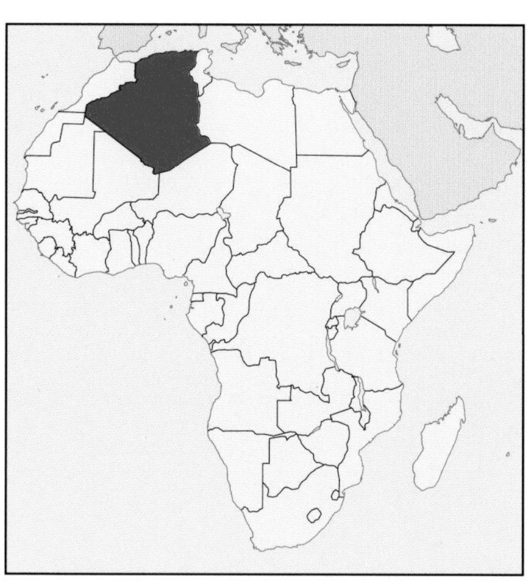

ANGOLA

Facts and Figures

Capital: Luanda 480,600 (1988)
Area (sq km): 1,246,700
Population: 10,770,000 (1993)
Language: Portuguese
Religion: Roman Catholic 75% Protestant 13% Traditional 16%
Currency: Kwanza = 100 lwei
Annual Income per person: $620
Annual Trade per person: $281
Adult Literacy: 42%
Life Expectancy (F): 48
Life Expectancy (M): 45

Location Map

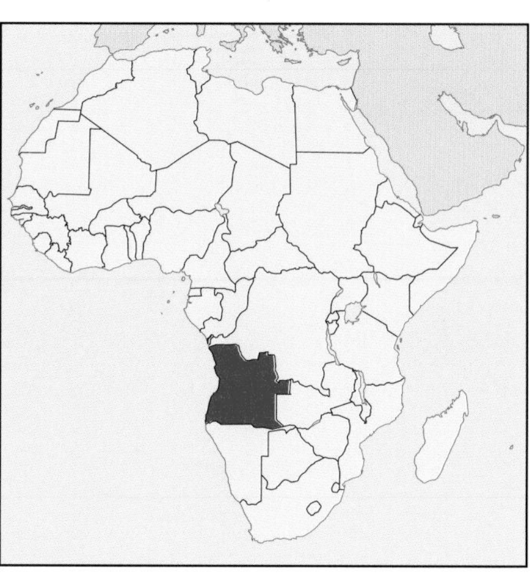

AZORES

Facts and Figures

Capital: Ponta Delgada 21,091 (1991)
Area (sq km): 2,247
Population: 260,000 (1991)
Language: Portuguese
Religion: Roman Catholic
Currency: Escudo
Annual Income per person: Data not available
Annual Trade per person: Data not available
Adult Literacy: Data not available
Life Expectancy (F): Data not available
Life Expectancy (M): Data not available

Location Map

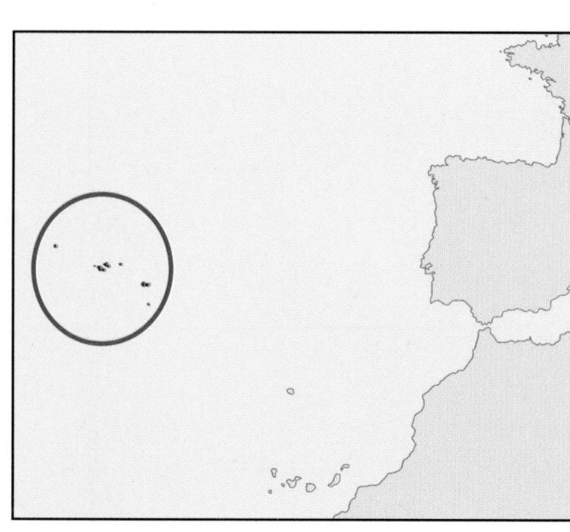

BENIN

Facts and Figures

Capital: Porto Novo 208,260 (1982)
Area (sq km): 112,620
Population: 5,010,000 (1993)
Language: French, Fon
Religion: Traditional 60% Roman Catholic 18% Sunni Muslim 15%
Currency: CFA Franc = 100 centimes
Annual Income per person: $380
Annual Trade per person: $156
Adult Literacy: 23%
Life Expectancy (F): 50
Life Expectancy (M): 46

Location Map

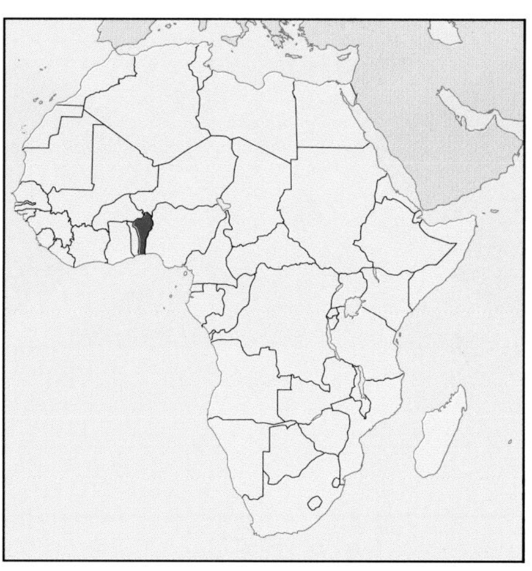

BOTSWANA

Facts and Figures

Capital: Gaborone 138,470 (1991)
Area (sq km): 581,730
Population: 1,330,000 (1991)
Language: English, Setswana
Religion: Traditional 50% Christian 30%
Currency: Pula = 100 thebe
Annual Income per person: $2,590
Annual Trade per person: $2,500
Adult Literacy: 74%
Life Expectancy (F): 64
Life Expectancy (M): 58

Location Map

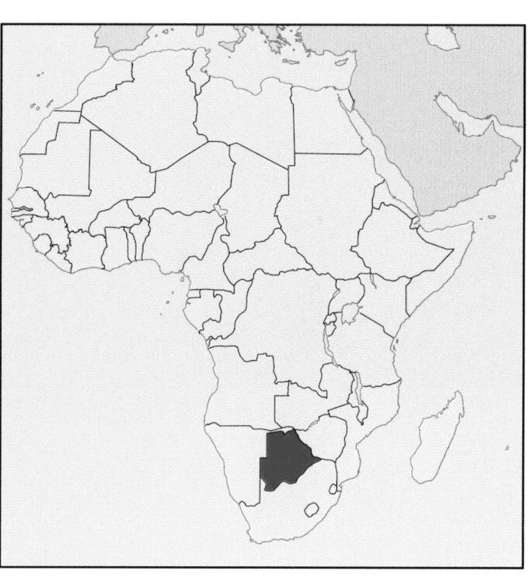

BURKINA FASO

Facts and Figures

Capital: Ouagadougou 442,230 (1985)
Area (sq km): 274,400
Population: 9,190,000 (1991)
Language: French
Religion: Sunni Muslim 52% Christian 21%
Currency: CFA Franc = 100 centimes
Annual Income per person: $350
Annual Trade per person: $48
Adult Literacy: 18%
Life Expectancy (F): 51
Life Expectancy (M): 48

Location Map

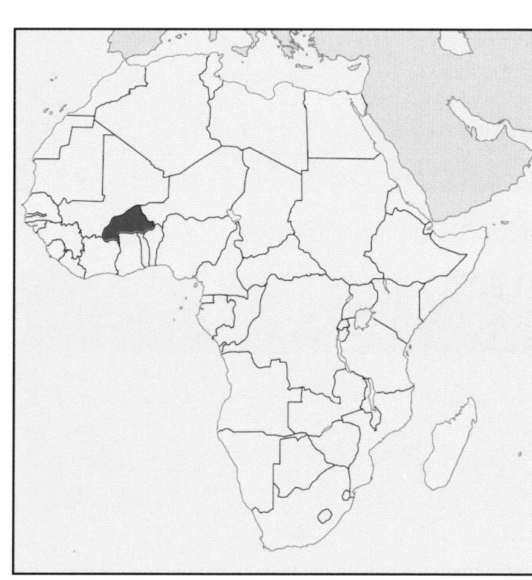

Flags of Africa

BURUNDI

Facts and Figures

Capital: Bujumbura 241,000 (1989)
Area (sq km): 27,830
Population: 5,600,000 (1992)
Language: French, Kirundi
Religion: Roman Catholic 62%
Traditional 30%
Currency: Burundi Franc = 100 centimes
Annual Income per person: $210
Annual Trade per person: $60
Adult Literacy: 50%
Life Expectancy (F): 51
Life Expectancy (M): 48

Location Map

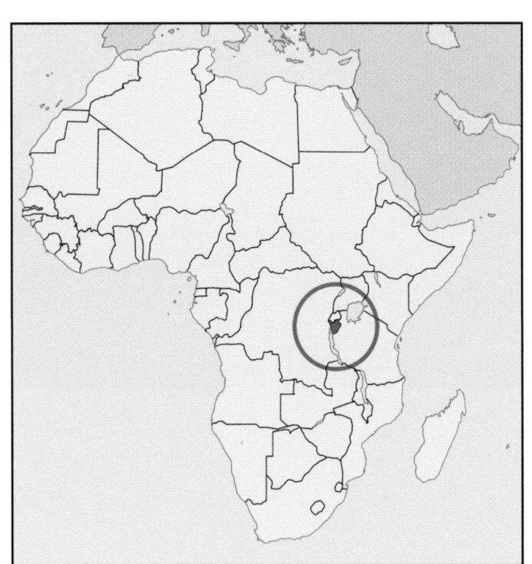

CAMEROON

Facts and Figures

Capital: Yaoundé 750,000 (1991)
Area (sq km): 475,442
Population: 12,240,000 (1991)
Language: French, English
Religion: Roman Catholic 28% Animist 25%
Sunni Muslim 22% Protestant 18%
Currency: CFA Franc = 100 centimes
Annual Income per person: $940
Annual Trade per person: $310
Adult Literacy: 54%
Life Expectancy (F): 57
Life Expectancy (M): 54

Location Map

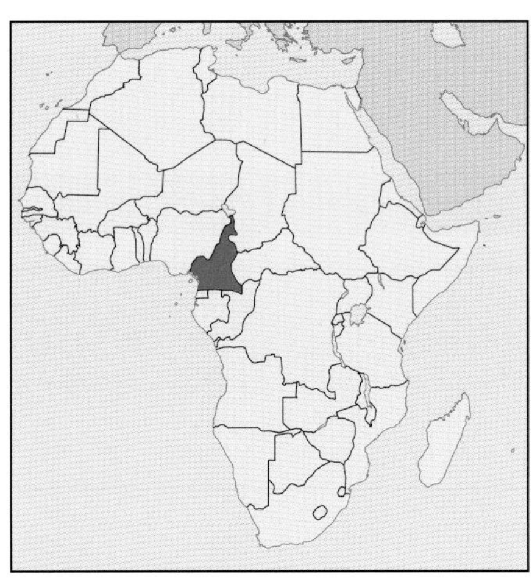

CAPE VERDE

Facts and Figures

Capital: Praia 61,700 (1990)
Area (sq km): 4,030
Population: 350,000 (1993)
Language: Portuguese, Crioulo
Religion: Roman Catholic 93% Protestant 7%
Currency: Escudo = 100 centavos
Annual Income per person: $750
Annual Trade per person: $331
Adult Literacy: 53 %
Life Expectancy (F): 69
Life Expectancy (M): 67

Location Map

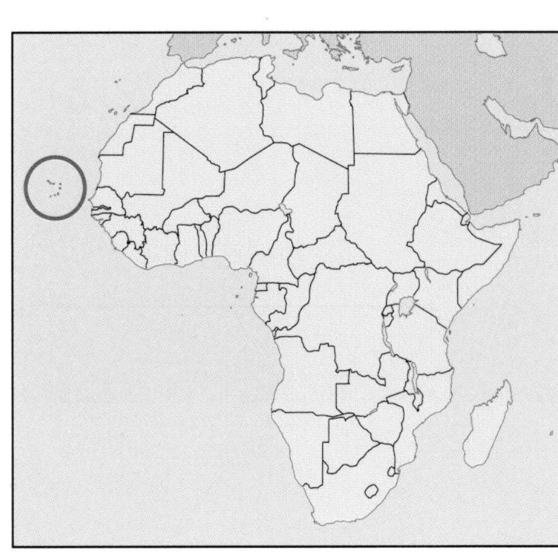

CENTRAL AFRICAN REPUBLIC

Facts and Figures

Capital: Bangui 451,700 (1988)
Area (sq km): 622,440
Population: 3,130,000 (1991)
Language: French, Sango
Religion: Protestant 45% Roman Catholic 30% Traditional
Currency: CFA Franc = 100 centimes
Annual Income per person: $390
Annual Trade per person: $70
Adult Literacy: 38%
Life Expectancy (F): 53
Life Expectancy (M): 48

Location Map

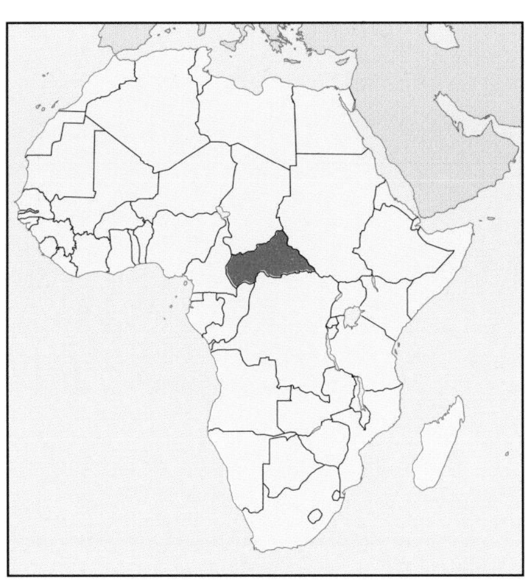

CHAD

Facts and Figures

Capital: N'Djaména 529,560 (1993)
Area (sq km): 1,284,000
Population: 6,290,000 (1993)
Language: French, Arabic
Religion: Muslim 41% Traditional 35% Christian 23%
Currency: CFA Franc = 100 centimes
Annual Income per person: $220
Annual Trade per person: $104
Adult Literacy: 30%
Life Expectancy (F): 49
Life Expectancy (M): 46

Location Map

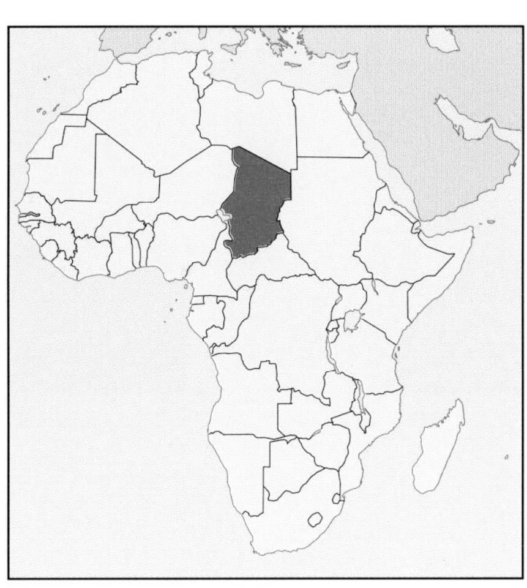

COMOROS

Facts and Figures

Capital: Moroni 22,000 (1992)
Area (sq km): 2,230
Population: 510,000 (1992)
Language: Swahili, French, Arabic
Religion: Sunni Muslim 93%
Currency: Comorian Franc
Annual Income per person: $500
Annual Trade per person: $120
Adult Literacy: 61%
Life Expectancy (F): 57
Life Expectancy (M): 56

Location Map

Flags of Africa

CONGO

Facts and Figures

Capital: Brazzaville 937,600 (1992)
Area (sq km): 341,800
Population: 2,690,000 (1992)
Language: French
Religion: Roman Catholic 46%
Protestant 19% Traditional
Currency: CFA Franc = 100 centimes
Annual Income per person: $1,120
Annual Trade per person: $694
Adult Literacy: 57%
Life Expectancy (F): 57
Life Expectancy (M): 52

Location Map

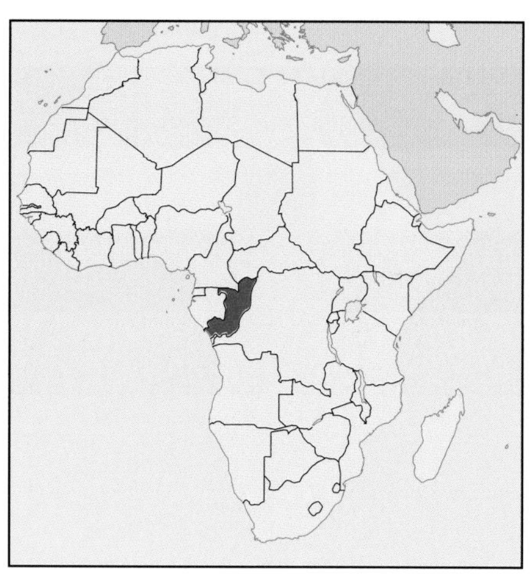

COTE D'IVOIRE

Facts and Figures

Capital: Yamoussoukro 120,000 (1986)
Area (sq km): 322,460
Population: 13,100,000 (1991)
Language: French
Religion: Muslim 20% Roman Catholic 20%
Traditional 44%
Currency: CFA Franc = 100 centimes
Annual Income per person: $690
Annual Trade per person: $443
Adult Literacy: 54%
Life Expectancy (F): 56
Life Expectancy (M): 53

Location Map

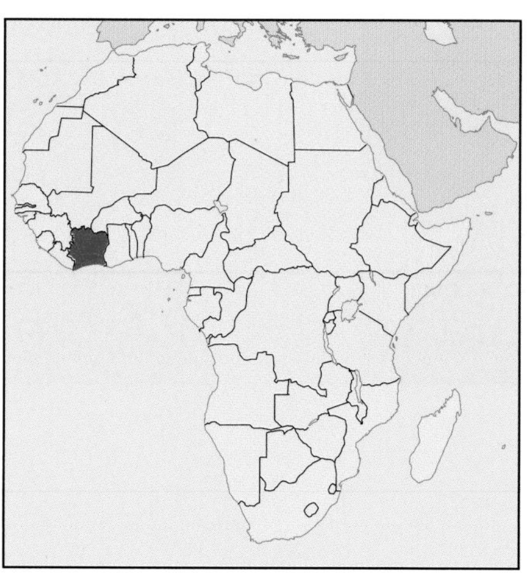

DJIBOUTI

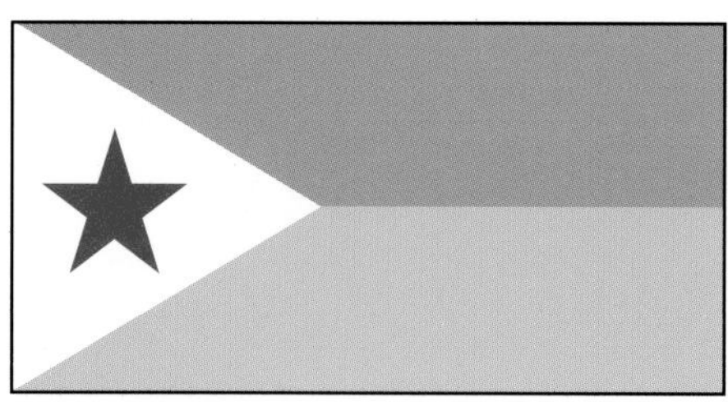

Facts and Figures

Capital: Djibouti 317,000 (1991)
Area (sq km): 23,200
Population: 542,000 (1991)
Language: Arabic, French, Cushitic
Religion: Sunni Muslim 94%
Roman Catholic 4%
Currency: Djibouti Franc
Annual Income per person: $1,000
Annual Trade per person: $550
Adult Literacy: 19%
Life Expectancy (F): 51
Life Expectancy (M): 47

Location Map

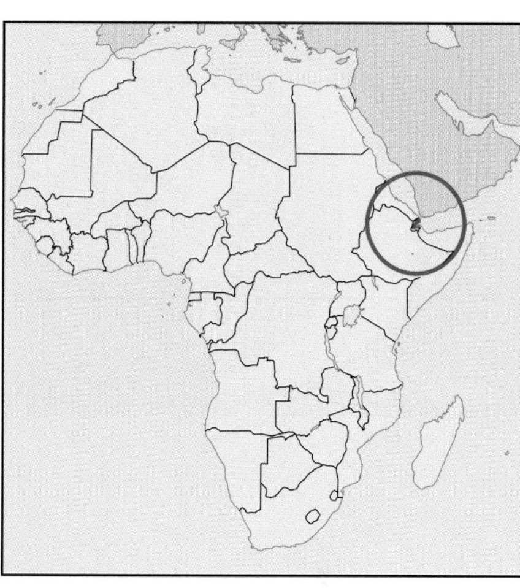

EGYPT

Facts and Figures

Capital: Cairo 6,663,000 (1991)
Area (sq km): 1,001,450
Population: 56,430,000 (1993)
Language: Arabic, French, English
Religion: Sunni Muslim 92% Christian
Currency: Egyptian Pound = 100 piastres
Annual Income per person: $620
Annual Trade per person: $211
Adult Literacy: 48%
Life Expectancy (F): 63
Life Expectancy (M): 60

Location Map

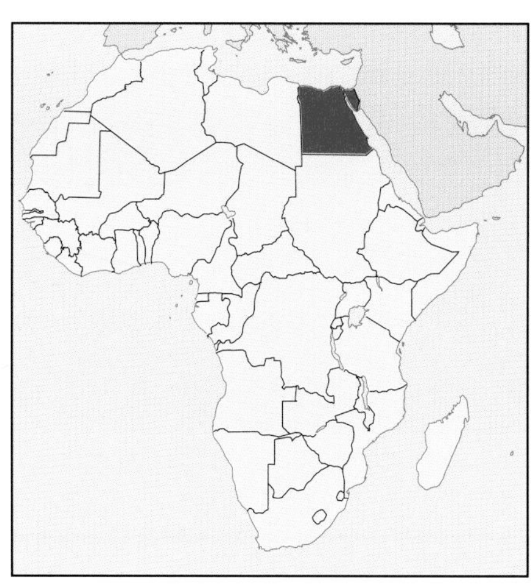

ERITREA

Facts and Figures

Capital: Asmara 367,300 (1991)
Area (sq km): 93,679
Population: 3,500,00 (1991)
Language: Tigrinya, Arabic
Religion: Muslim 50% Coptic Christian 50%
Currency: Ethiopean birr = 100 cents
Annual Income per person: Data not available
Annual Trade per person: Data not available
Adult Literacy: Data not available
Life Expectancy (F): Data not available
Life Expectancy (M): Data not available

Location Map

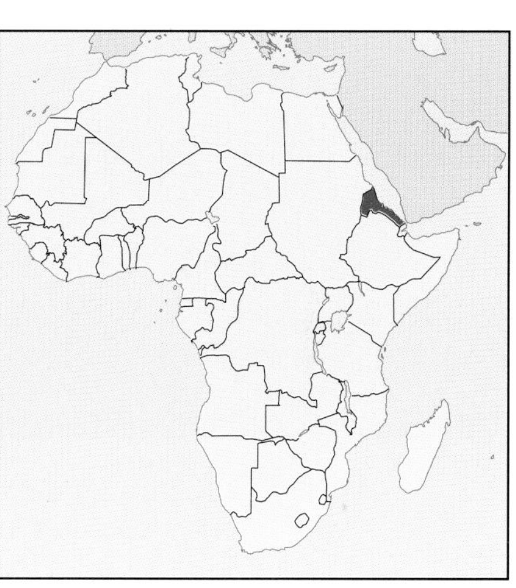

ETHIOPIA

Facts and Figures

Capital: Addis Ababa 1,700,000 (1990)
Area (sq km): 1,157,603
Population: 51,980,000 (1993)
Language: Amharic, Galla, Tigre
Religion: Muslim 45%, Christian 40%, Traditional 12%
Currency: Ethiopean birr = 100 cents
Annual Income per person: $120
Annual Trade per person: $12
Adult Literacy: 66%
Life Expectancy (F): 49
Life Expectancy (M): 45

Location Map

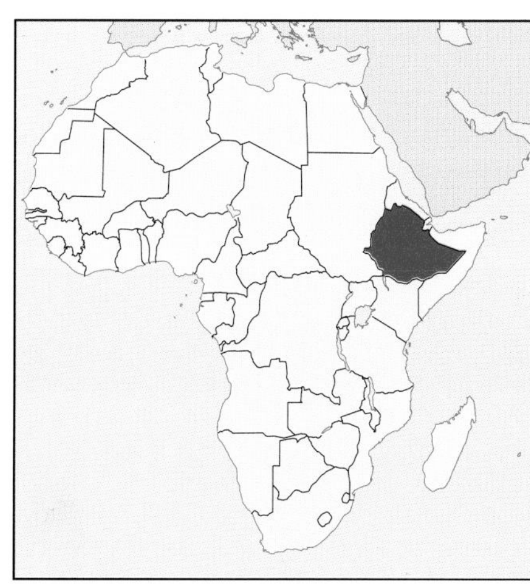

Flags of Africa

EQUATORIAL GUINEA

Facts and Figures

Capital: Malabo 370,000 (1988)
Area (sq km): 28,051
Population: 417,000 (1990)
Language: Spanish, Fang
Religion: Roman Catholic 89%
Currency: CFA Franc = 100 centimes
Annual Income per person: $330
Annual Trade per person: $250
Adult Literacy: 50%
Life Expectancy (F): 50
Life Expectancy (M): 46

Location Map

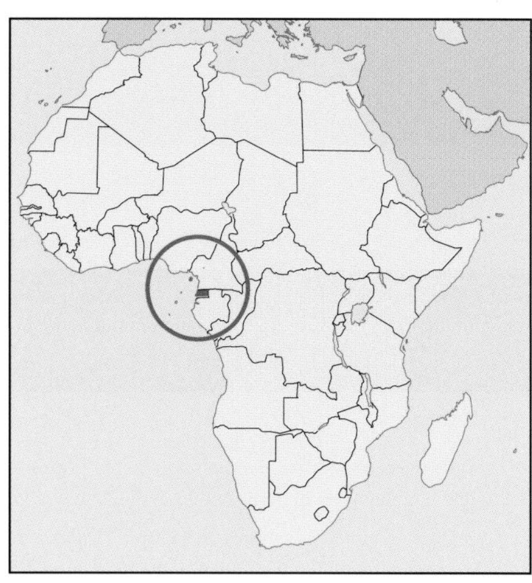

GABON

Facts and Figures

Capital: Libreville 350,000 (1983)
Area (sq km): 267,670
Population: 1,010,000 (1993)
Language: French, Bantu
Religion: Roman Catholic 75%, Traditional
Currency: CFA Franc = 100 centimes
Annual Income per person: $3,780
Annual Trade per person: $2,094
Adult Literacy: 61%
Life Expectancy (F): 55
Life Expectancy (M): 52

Location Map

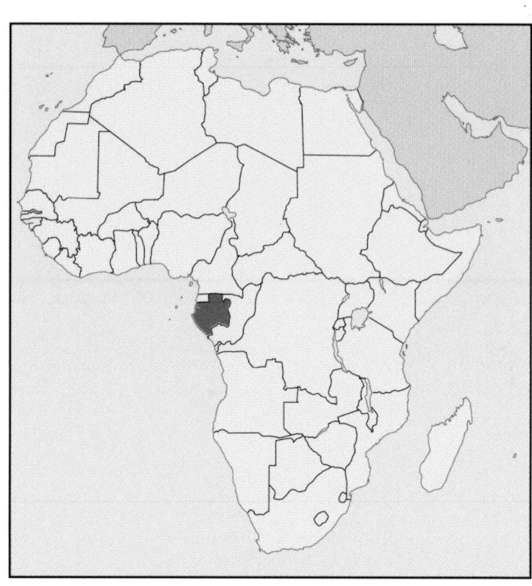

GAMBIA

Facts and Figures

Capital: Banjul 52,000 (1992)
Area (sq km): 11,300
Population: 875,000 (1990)
Language: English, Madinka
Religion: Sunni Muslim 95% Christian 4%
Currency: Dalasi = 100 butut
Annual Income per person: $360
Annual Trade per person: $298
Adult Literacy: 27%
Life Expectancy (F): 47
Life Expectancy (M): 43

Location Map

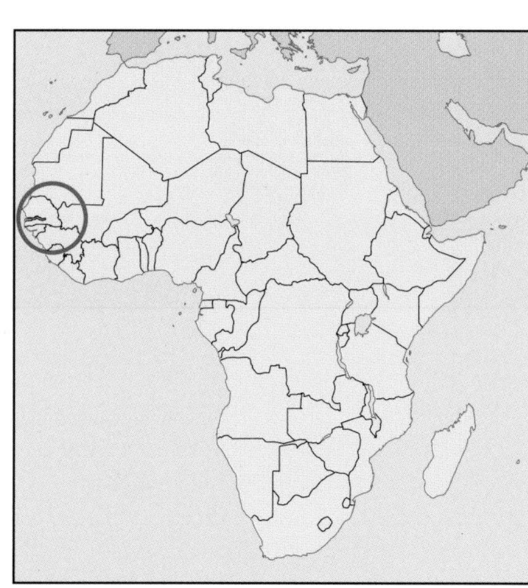

GHANA

Facts and Figures

Capital: Accra 1,050,000 (1992)
Area (sq km): 238,540
Population: 16,700,000 (1991)
Language: English ,Akan ,Mossi, Ewe, Ga-Adangme
Religion: Protestant 28% Traditional 21% Roman Catholic 19% Muslim 16%
Currency: Cedi = 100 pesewas
Annual Income per person: $400
Annual Trade per person: $158
Adult Literacy: 60%
Life Expectancy (F): 58
Life Expectancy (M): 54

Location Map

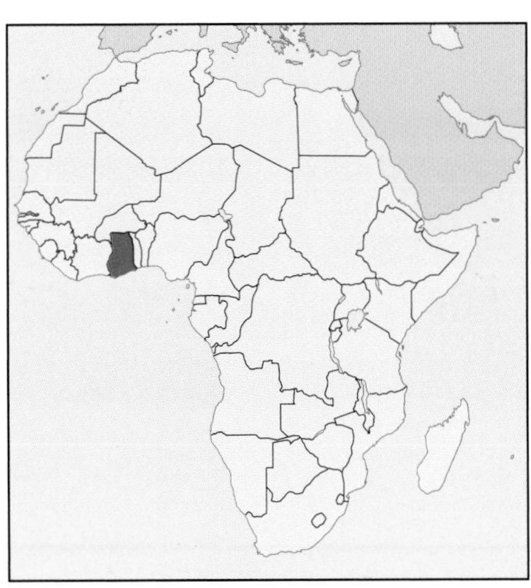

GUINEA

Facts and Figures

Capital: Conakry 860,000 (1992)
Area (sq km): 245,860
Population: 7,300,000 (1990)
Language: French, Susu, Fulani, Malinké
Religion: Muslim 69% Traditional 30%
Currency: Guinean Franc = 100 cauris
Annual Income per person: $450
Annual Trade per person: $160
Adult Literacy: 24%
Life Expectancy (F): 45
Life Expectancy (M): 44

Location Map

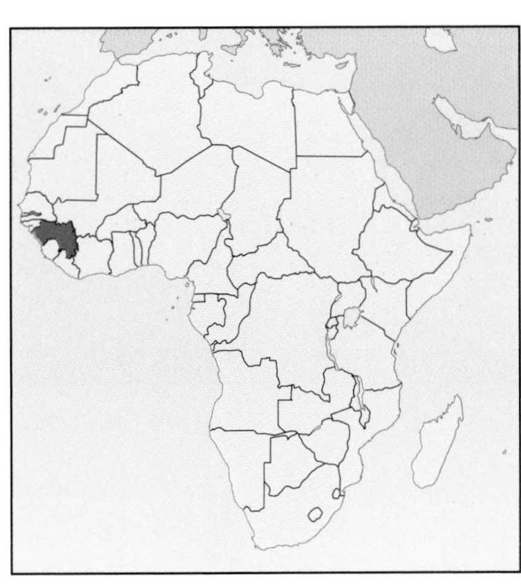

GUINEA BISSAU

Facts and Figures

Capital: Bissau 135,000 (1992)
Area (sq km): 36,125
Population: 980,000 (1991)
Language: Portuguese, Crioulo
Religion: Traditional 65% Muslim 30%
Currency: Peso = 100 centavos
Annual Income per person: $190
Annual Trade per person: $85
Adult Literacy: 36%
Life Expectancy (F): 45
Life Expectancy (M): 42

Location Map

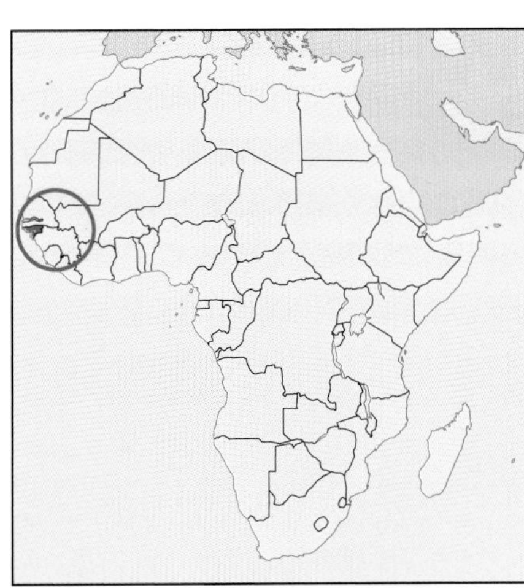

Flags of Africa

KENYA

Facts and Figures

Capital: Nairobi 1,500,000 (1992)
Area (sq km): 582,650
Population: 27,900,000 (1991)
Language: Swahili, Kikuyu, English
Religion: Roman Catholic 23%
Other Christian 23% Protestant 15%
Traditional 15%
Currency: Kenya shilling =100cents
Annual Income per person: $340
Annual Trade per person: $113
Adult Literacy: 69%
Life Expectancy (F): 63
Life Expectancy (M): 59

Location Map

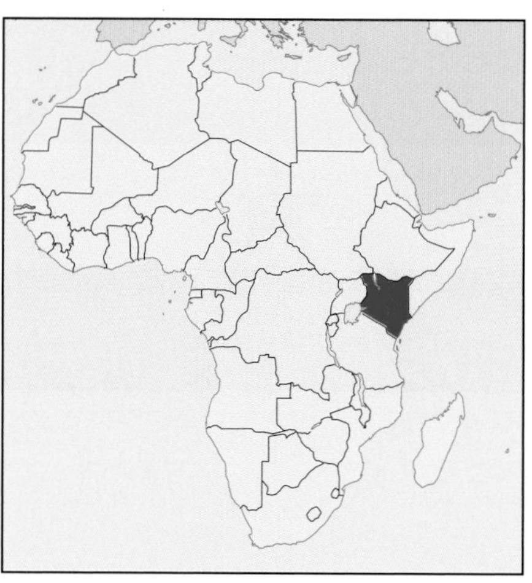

LESOTHO

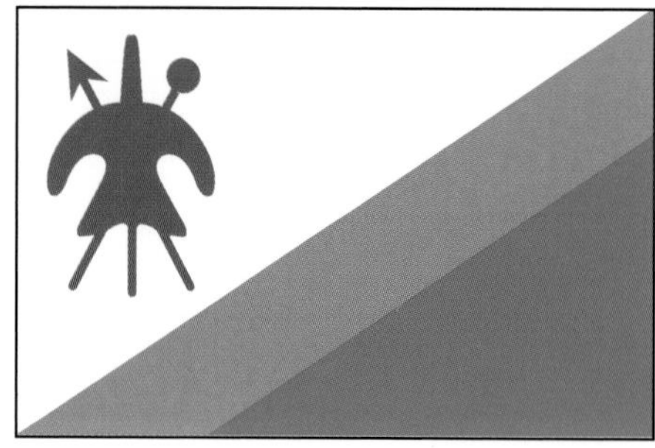

Facts and Figures

Capital: Maseru 126,000 (1992)
Area (sq km): 30,355
Population: 1,830,000 (1991)
Language: Sesotho,English
Religion: Protestant 49% Roman Catholic 44%
Currency: Loti = 100 lisente
Annual Income per person: $580
Annual Trade per person: $350
Adult Literacy: 60%
Life Expectancy (F): 63
Life Expectancy (M): 54

Location Map

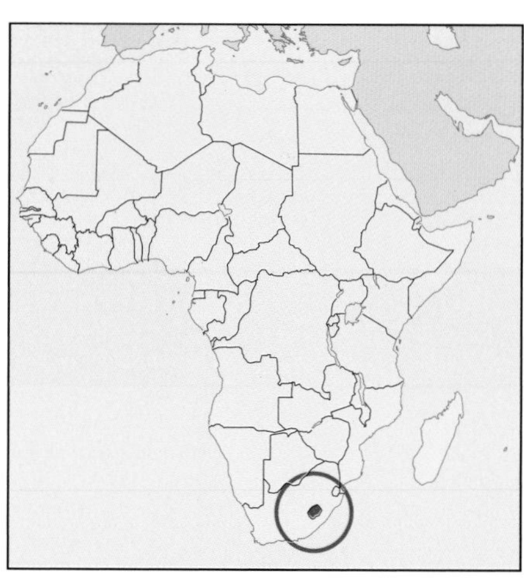

LIBERIA

Facts and Figures

Capital: Monrovia 540,000 (1992)
Area (sq km): 99,070
Population: 2,830,000 (1992)
Language: English, Mande, West Atlantic ,Kwa
Religion: Sunni Muslim 30% Protestant 15%
Roman Catholic 5%
Currency: Liberian Dollar
Annual Income per person: $600
Annual Trade per person: $285
Adult Literacy: 40%
Life Expectancy (F): 57
Life Expectancy (M): 54

Location Map

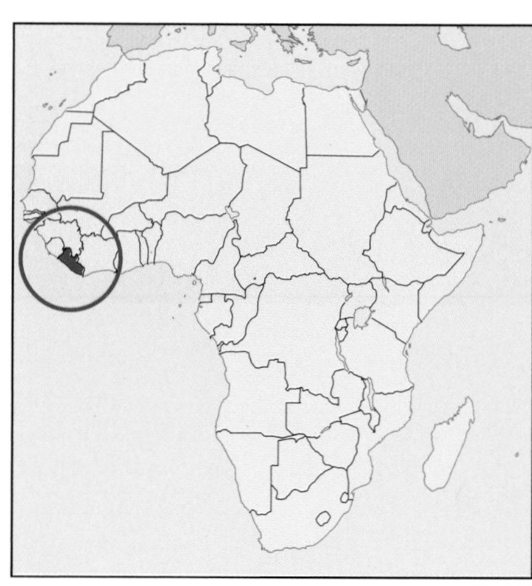

LIBYA

Facts and Figures

Capital: Tripoli 858,000 (1981)
Area (sq km): 1,759,540
Population: 4,700,000 (1990)
Language: Arabic, Berber
Religion: Sunni Muslim 97%
Currency: Libyan dinar = 1000 millemes
Annual Income per person: $5,500
Annual Trade per person: $3,332
Adult Literacy: 64%
Life Expectancy (F): 65
Life Expectancy (M): 62

Location Map

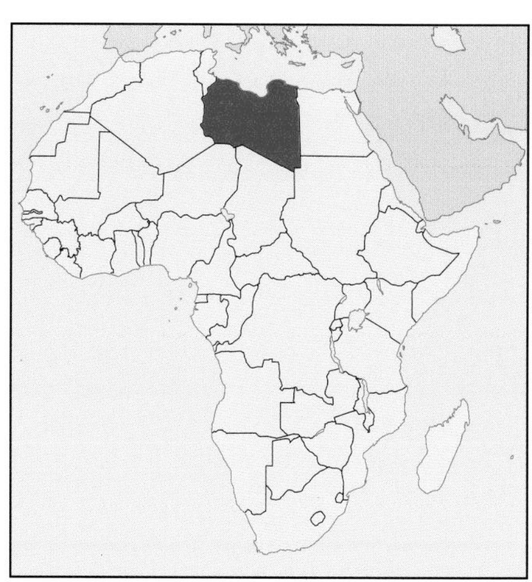

MADAGASCAR

Facts and Figures

Capital: Antananarivo 1,803,390 (1990)
Area (sq km): 587,040
Population: 12,370,000 (1991)
Language: Malagasy, French, English
Religion: Traditional 47%
Roman Catholic 26%
Protestant 22%
Currency: Malagasy Franc = 100 centimes
Annual Income per person: $210
Annual Trade per person: $65
Adult Literacy: 80%
Life Expectancy (F): 57
Life Expectancy (M): 54

Location Map

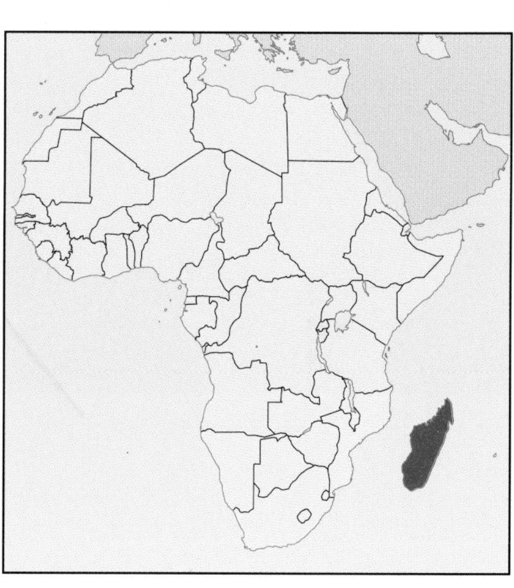

MALAWI

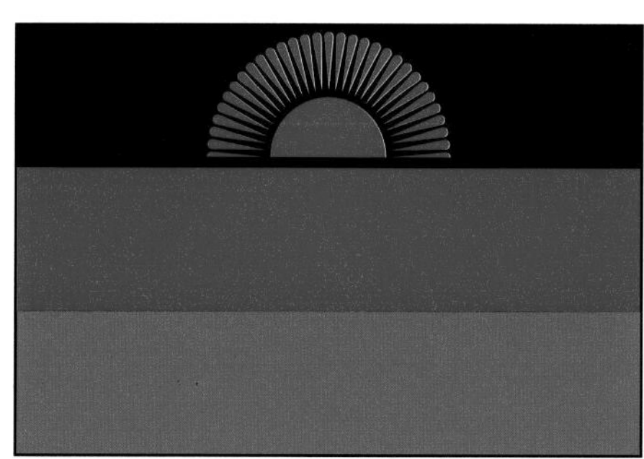

Facts and Figures

Capital: Lilongwe 275,000 (1992)
Area (sq km): 118,480
Population: 9,700,000 (1991)
Language: Chichewe, English
Religion: Protestant 64%
Roman Catholic 17% Muslim 12%
Currency: Kwacha = 100 tambala
Annual Income per person: $230
Annual Trade per person: $138
Adult Literacy: 22%
Life Expectancy (F): 50
Life Expectancy (M): 48

Location Map

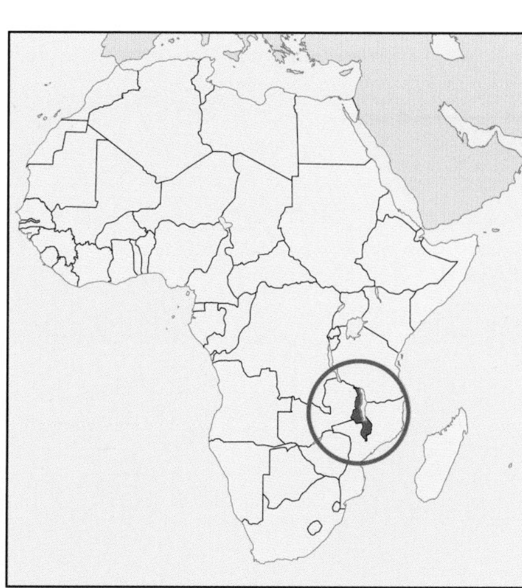

Flags of Africa

MALI

Facts and Figures

Capital: Bamako 745,000 (1992)
Area (sq km): 1,240,000
Population: 9,362,000 (1990)
Language: French, Bambara
Religion: Sunni Muslim 90% Traditional 9%
Currency: CFA Franc = 100 centimes
Annual Income per person: $280
Annual Trade per person: $97
Adult Literacy: 33%
Life Expectancy (F): 48
Life Expectancy (M): 40

Location Map

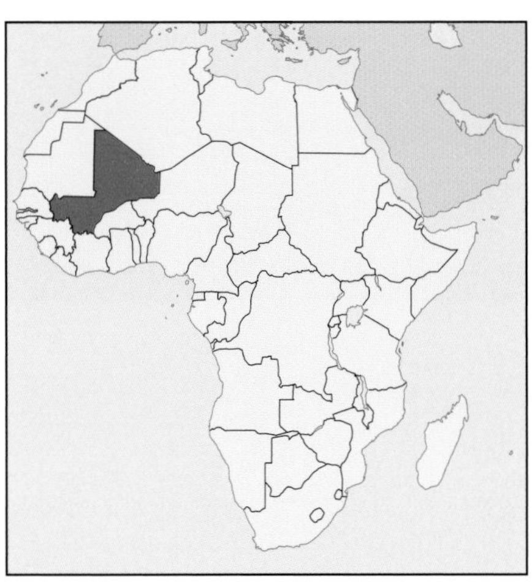

MAURITANIA

Facts and Figures

Capital: Nouakchott 440,600 (1992)
Area (sq km): 1,025,520
Population: 2,110,000 (1992)
Language: Arabic, French, Pulaar, Soninke, Wolof
Religion: Sunni Muslim 99%
Currency: Ouguiya = 5 khoumi
Annual Income per person: $510
Annual Trade per person: $335
Adult Literacy: 34%
Life Expectancy (F): 50
Life Expectancy (M): 46

Location Map

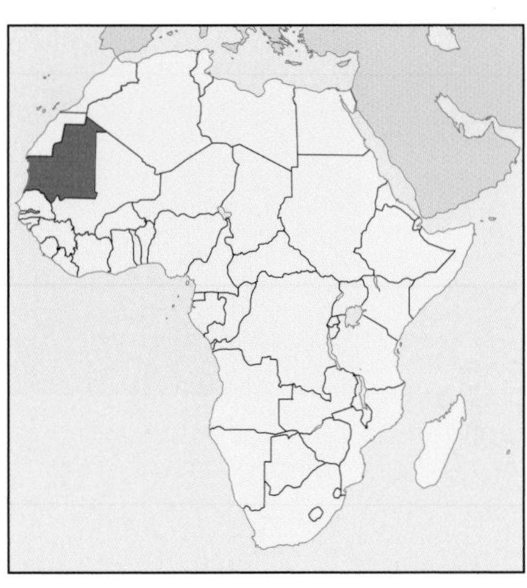

MAURITIUS

Facts and Figures

Capital: Port Louis 143,000 (1992)
Area (sq km): 2,040
Population: 1,092,400 (1992)
Language: English, Creole ,Hindi, French
Religion: Hindu 49% Roman Catholic 26% Muslim 16%
Currency: Mauritius Rupee = 100 cents
Annual Income per person: $2,420
Annual Trade per person: $2,586
Adult Literacy: 83%
Life Expectancy (F): 73
Life Expectancy (M): 68

Location Map

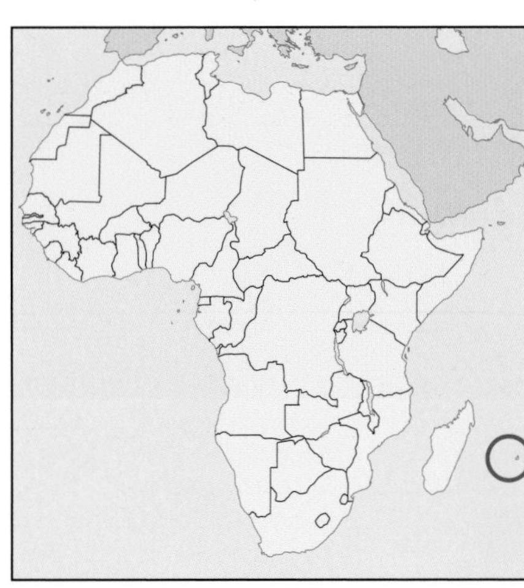

MOROCCO

Facts and Figures

Capital: Rabat 650,000 (1982)
Area (sq km): 458,730
Population: 25,700,00 (1991)
Language: Arabic, Berber
Religion: Sunni Muslim 98%
Currency: Dirham = 100 centimes
Annual Income per person: $1,030
Annual Trade per person: $434
Adult Literacy: 50%
Life Expectancy (F): 65
Life Expectancy (M): 62

Location Map

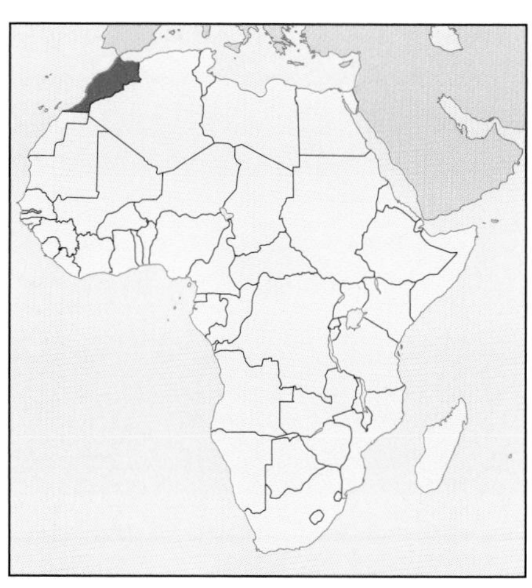

MOZAMBIQUE

Facts and Figures

Capital: Maputo 1,098,000 (1991)
Area (sq km): 799,380
Population: 16,110,000 (1991)
Language: Portuguese, Bantu
Religion: Traditional 60%
Roman Catholic 18% Muslim 13%
Currency: Metical = 100 centavos
Annual Income per person: $70
Annual Trade per person: $66
Adult Literacy: 35%
Life Expectancy (F): 50
Life Expectancy (M): 47

Location Map

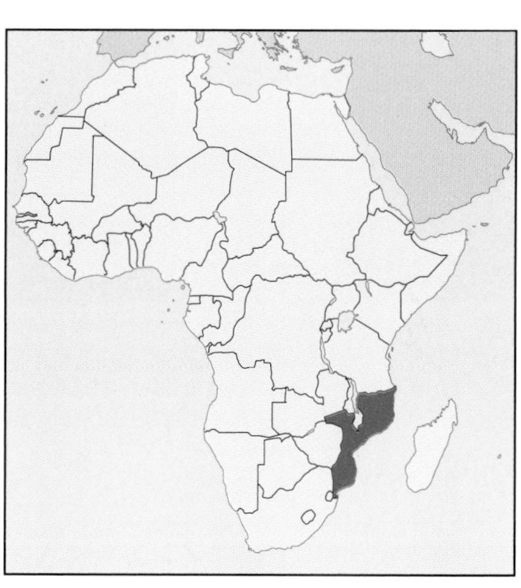

NAMIBIA

Facts and Figures

Capital: Windhoek 159,000 (1991)
Area (sq km): 824,270
Population: 1,510,000 (1992)
Language: English,Afrikaans,German
Religion: Lutheran 51% Other Christian 49%
Animist
Currency: Namibia $ and South African Rand
Annual Income per person: $1,120
Annual Trade per person: $1,200
Adult Literacy: 38%
Life Expectancy (F): 60
Life Expectancy (M): 58

Location Map

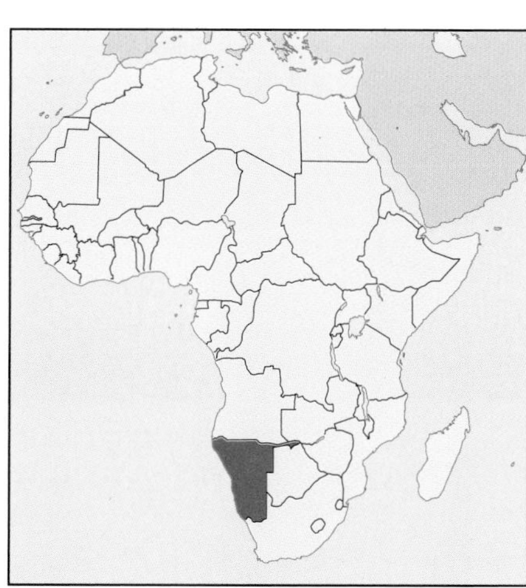

Flags of Africa

NIGER

Facts and Figures

Capital: Niamey 450,000 (1992)
Area (sq km): 1,267,000
Population: 8,040,000 (1991)
Language: French, Hausa
Religion: Sunni Muslim 71% Christian Traditional
Currency: CFA Franc = 100 centimes
Annual Income per person: $300
Annual Trade per person: $87
Adult Literacy: 29%
Life Expectancy (F): 48
Life Expectancy (M): 45

Location Map

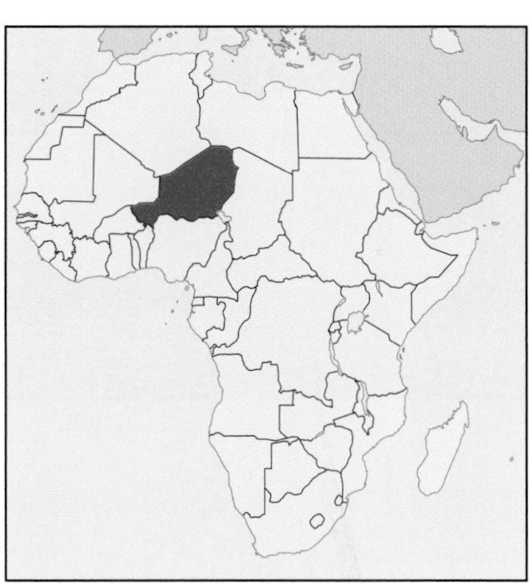

NIGERIA

Facts and Figures

Capital: Abuja 305,900 (1992)
Area (sq km): 923,770
Population: 92,800,000 (1991)
Language: English, Hausa, Ibo, Yoruba
Religion: Muslim 48% Protestant 17% Roman Catholic 17% Traditional
Currency: Naira =100 kobo
Annual Income per person: $290
Annual Trade per person: $159
Adult Literacy: 51%
Life Expectancy (F): 54
Life Expectancy (M): 51

Location Map

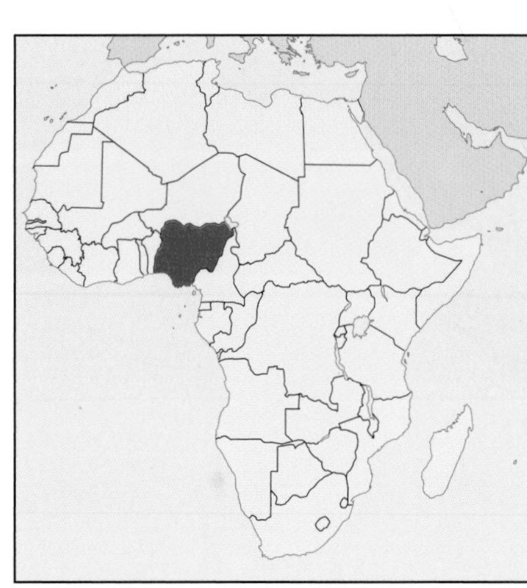

RWANDA

Facts and Figures

Capital: Kigali 156,650 (1981)
Area (sq km): 26,340
Population: 7,430,000 (1991)
Language: Kinyarwanda, French, Kiswahili, Watusi
Religion: Roman Catholic 61% Protestant 9% Muslim 9% Traditional
Currency: Rwanda Franc = 100 centimes
Annual Income per person: $260
Annual Trade per person: $70
Adult Literacy: 50%
Life Expectancy (F): 52
Life Expectancy (M): 49

Location Map

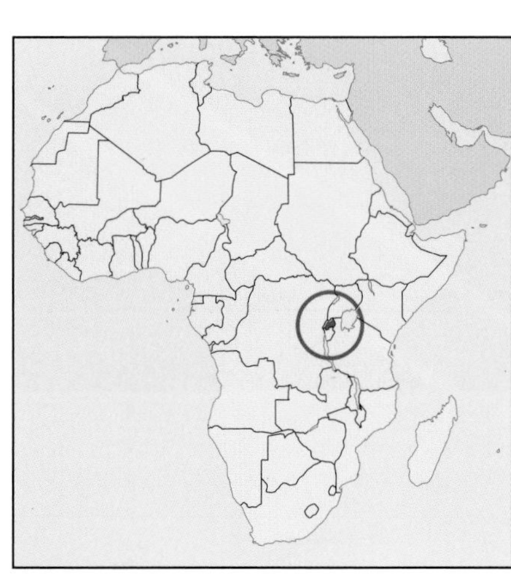

SAO TOME & PRINCIPE

Facts and Figures

Capital: São Tomé 35,000 (1984)
Area (sq km): 1,001
Population: 124,000 (1991)
Language: Portugese, Fang
Religion: Roman Catholic 80%
Currency: Dobra = 100 centimos
Annual Income per person: $350
Annual Trade per person: $200
Adult Literacy: 63%
Life Expectancy (F): 68
Life Expectancy (M): 64

Location Map

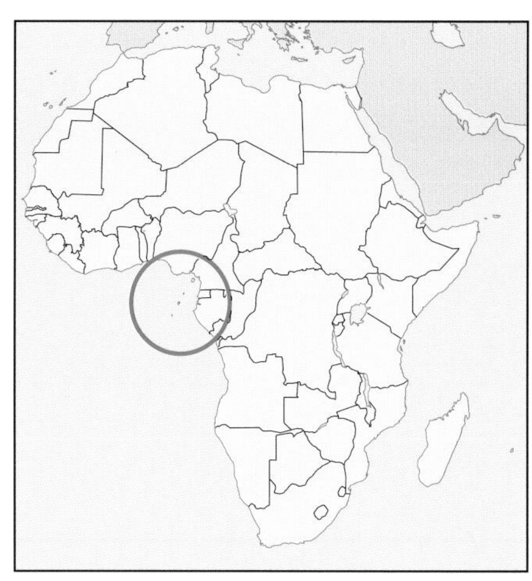

SENEGAL

Facts and Figures

Capital: Dakar 1,730,000 (1992)
Area (sq km): 197,160
Population: 7,970,000 (1993)
Language: French, Wolof
Religion: Sunni Muslim 91% Christian Animist
Currency: CFA Franc = centimes
Annual Income per person: $720
Annual Trade per person: $235
Adult Literacy: 38%
Life Expectancy (F): 50
Life Expectancy (M): 48

Location Map

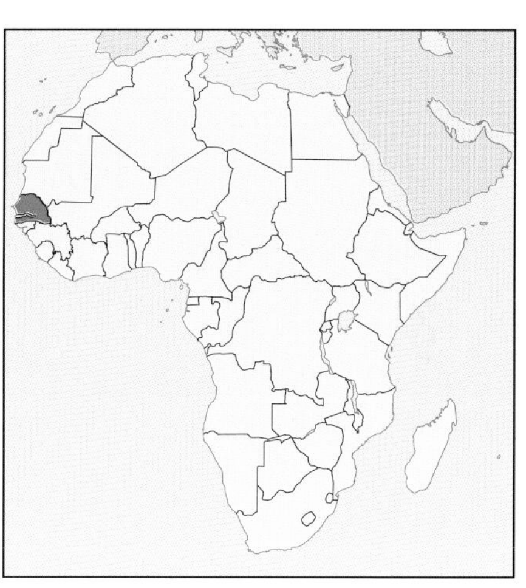

SEYCHELLES

Facts and Figures

Capital: Victoria 24,000 (1992)
Area (sq km): 455
Population: 80,000 (1991)
Language: English, French, Creole
Religion: Roman Catholic 92%
Currency: Seychelles Rupee = 100 cents
Annual Income per person: $5,110
Annual Trade per person: $3,157
Adult Literacy: 89%
Life Expectancy (F): 75
Life Expectancy (M): 65

Location Map

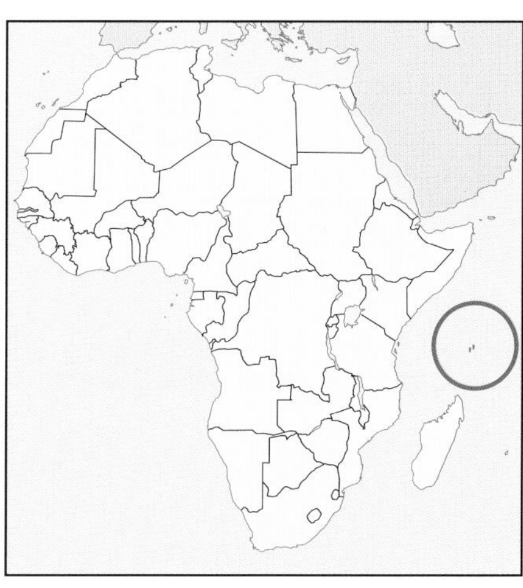

Flags of Africa

SIERRA LEONE

Facts and Figures

Capital: Freetown 550,000 (1992)
Area (sq km): 73,330
Population: 4,260,000 (1991)
Language: English, Creole
Religion: Traditional 52% Muslim 39% Christian
Currency: Leone =100cents
Annual Income per person: $210
Annual Trade per person: $72
Adult Literacy: 21%
Life Expectancy (F): 45
Life Expectancy (M): 41

Location Map

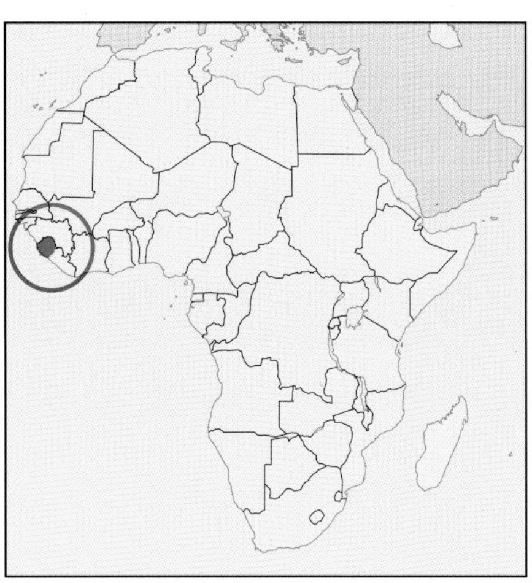

SOMALIA

Facts and Figures

Capital: Mogadishu 485,000 (1992)
Area (sq km): 637,660
Population: 8,000,000 (1990)
Language: Somali, Arabic ,English, Italian
Religion: Sunni Muslim 99%
Currency: Somali Shilling = 100 cents
Annual Income per person: $150
Annual Trade per person: $35
Adult Literacy: 25%
Life Expectancy (F): 49
Life Expectancy (M): 45

Location Map

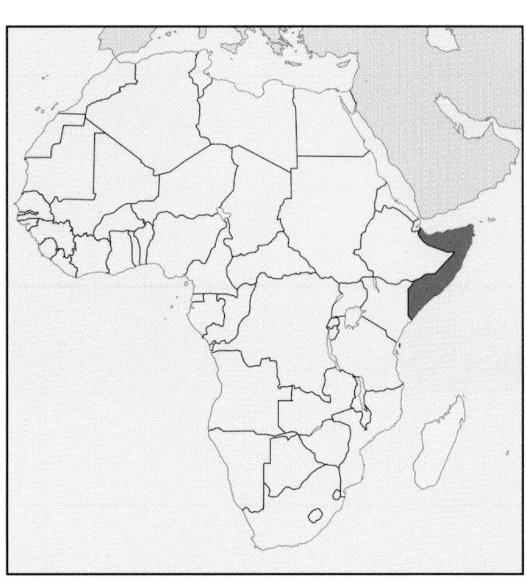

SOUTH AFRICA

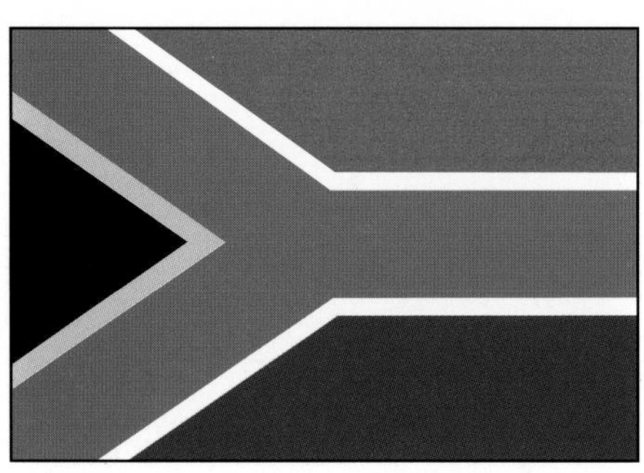

Facts and Figures

Capital: Pretoria 525,600 (1991)
Area (sq km): 1,126,771
Population: 42,500,000 (1993)
Language: Afrikaans, English, Xhosa ,Zulu
Religion: Black Christian 42%
Dutch Reform 23%
Roman Catholic 15%
Currency: Rand = 100 cents
Annual Income per person: $2,600
Annual Trade per person: $964
Adult Literacy: 70%
Life Expectancy (F): 66
Life Expectancy (M): 60

Location Map

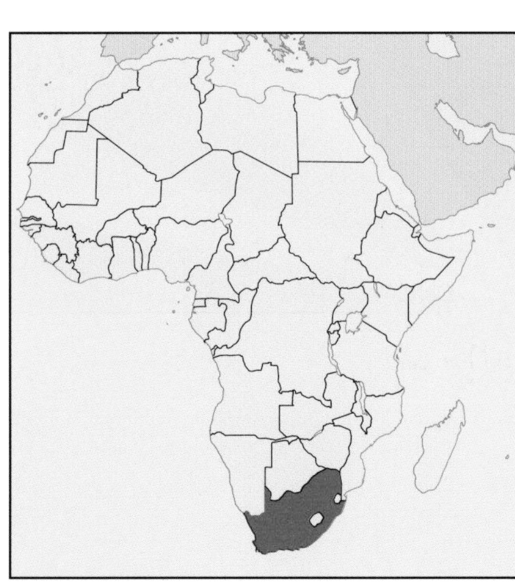

SUDAN

Facts and Figures

Capital: Khartoum 625,000 (1992)
Area (sq km): 2,505,810
Population: 30,830,000 (1993)
Language: Arabic, Nubian, English
Religion: Sunni Muslim 71% Traditional 16% Christian 8%
Currency: Dinar = 100 piastres
Annual Income per person: $450
Annual Trade per person: $66
Adult Literacy: 27%
Life Expectancy (F): 53
Life Expectancy (M): 51

Location Map

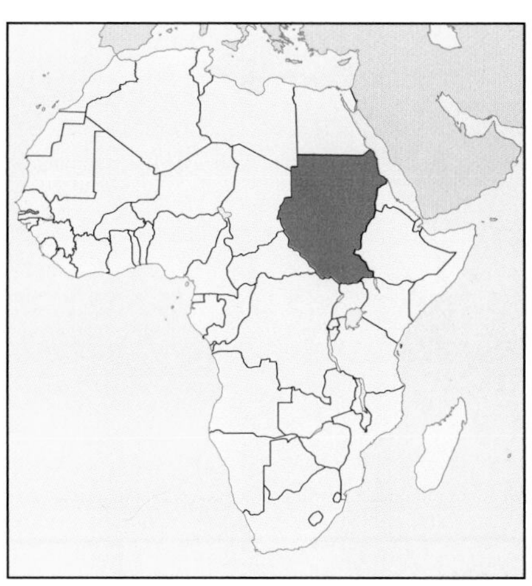

SWAZILAND

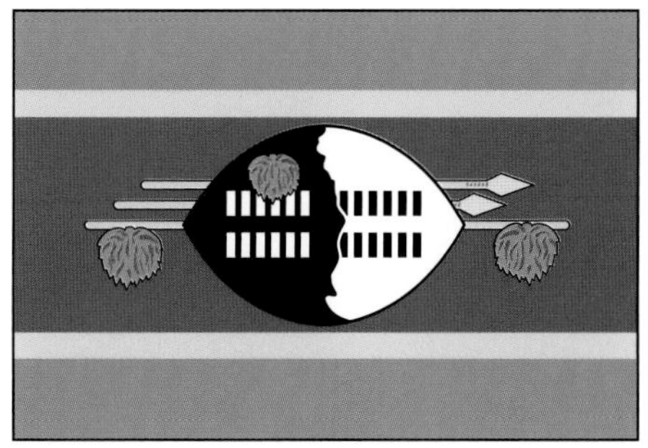

Facts and Figures

Capital: Mbabane 45,000 (1992)
Area (sq km): 17,360
Population: 835,000 (1989)
Language: Swazi, English
Religion: Christian 60% Traditional 40%
Currency: Lilangeni = 100 cents
Annual Income per person: $1,060
Annual Trade per person: $1,300
Adult Literacy: 72%
Life Expectancy (F): 60
Life Expectancy (M): 56

Location Map

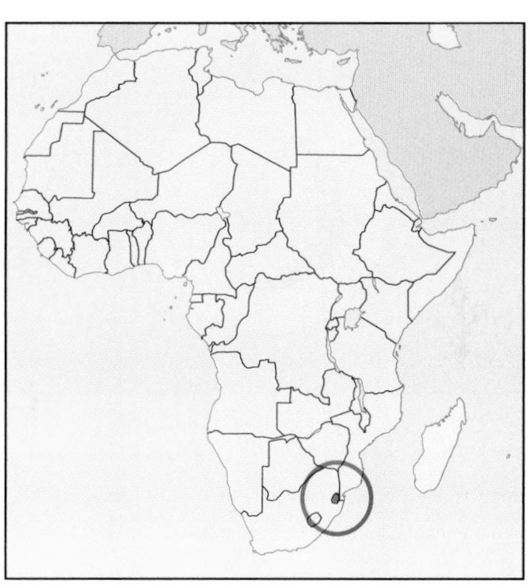

TANZANIA

Facts and Figures

Capital: Dodoma 225,000 (1992)
Area (sq km): 945,090
Population: 28,200,000 (1991)
Language: Swahili, English
Religion: Christian 40% Muslim 33% Traditional 23%
Currency: Tanzanian Shilling = 100 cents
Annual Income per person: $100
Annual Trade per person: $56
Adult Literacy: 65%
Life Expectancy (F): 55
Life Expectancy (M): 50

Location Map

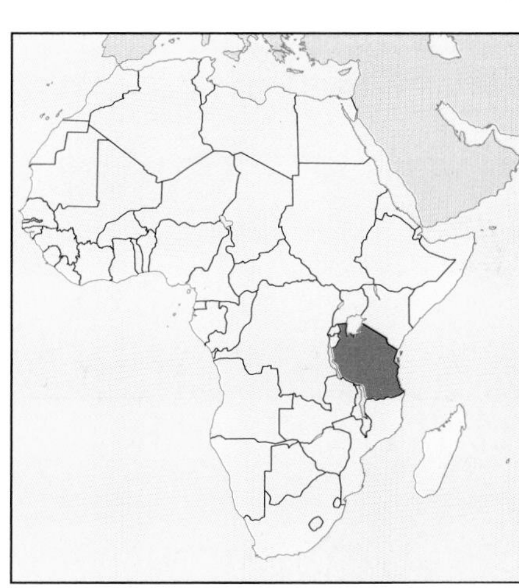

Flags of Africa

TOGO

Facts and Figures

Capital: Lomé 500,000 (1987)
Area (sq km): 56,790
Population: 4,100,000 (1991)
Language: French, Ewe, Kabiye
Religion: Traditional 50%
Roman Catholic 26% Muslim 15%
Protestant 9%
Currency: CFA Franc = 100 centimes
Annual Income per person: $400
Annual Trade per person: $210
Adult Literacy: 43%
Life Expectancy (F): 57
Life Expectancy (M): 53

Location Map

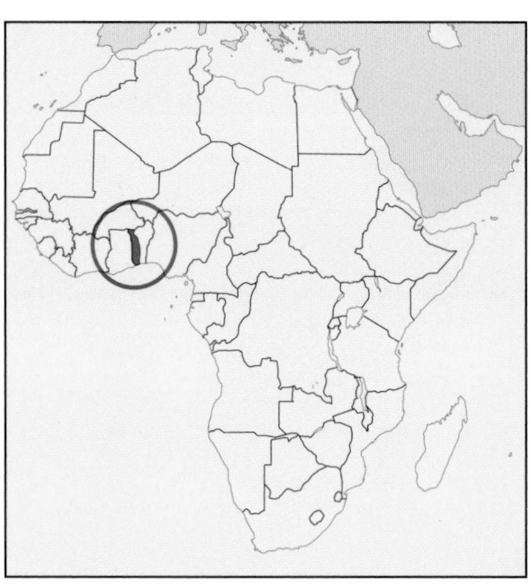

TUNISIA

Facts and Figures

Capital: Tunis 687,000 (1992)
Area (sq km): 164,150
Population: 8,370,000 (1992)
Language: Arabic, French
Religion: Muslim 97%
Currency: Tunisian Dinar = 1000 millimes
Annual Income per person: $1,510
Annual Trade per person: $1,065
Adult Literacy: 65%
Life Expectancy (F): 69
Life Expectancy (M): 67

Location Map

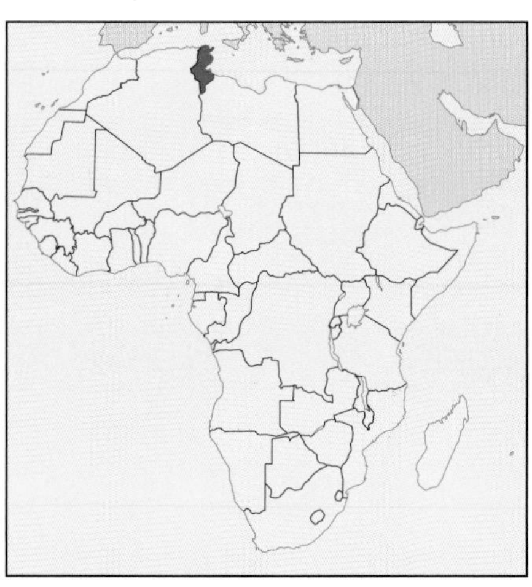

UGANDA

Facts and Figures

Capital: Kampala 773,500 (1991)
Area (sq km): 241,040
Population: 19,600,000 (1991)
Language: English, Swahili, Bantu languages
Religion: Roman Catholic 40%
Protestant 29% Traditional 18%
Muslim 7%
Currency: Uganda Shilling = 100 cents
Annual Income per person: $170
Annual Trade per person: $20
Adult Literacy: 48%
Life Expectancy (F): 55
Life Expectancy (M): 51

Location Map

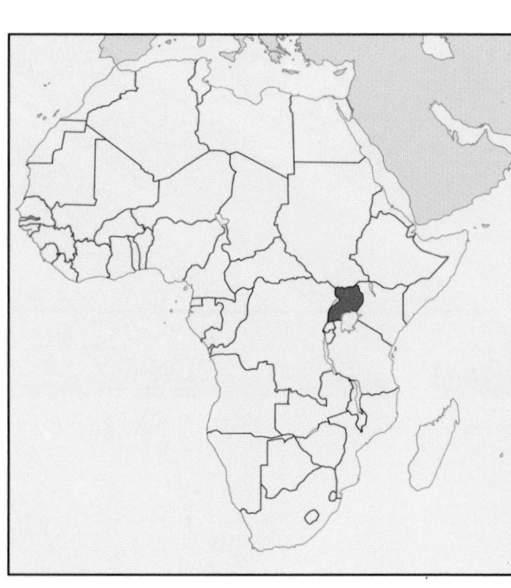

DEMOCRATIC REPUBLIC OF CONGO

Facts and Figures

Capital: Kinshasa 3,330,000 (1992)
Area (sq km): 2,344,890
Population: 40,256,000 (1991)
Language: French, Swahili, Tshiluba, Kikongo, Lingala
Religion: Roman Catholic 47% Protestant 28% Kimbanguiste 17%
Currency: New Zaire = 100 makuta
Annual Income per person: $220
Annual Trade per person: $42
Adult Literacy: 72%
Life Expectancy (F): 56
Life Expectancy (M): 52

Location Map

ZAMBIA

Facts and Figures

Capital: Lusaka 950,000 (1992)
Area (sq km): 752,610
Population: 8,780,000 (1991)
Language: English, Bantu languages
Religion: Christian 67% Traditional
Currency: Kwacha = 100 negwee
Annual Income per person: $420
Annual Trade per person: $265
Adult Literacy: 73%
Life Expectancy (F): 57
Life Expectancy (M): 54

Location Map

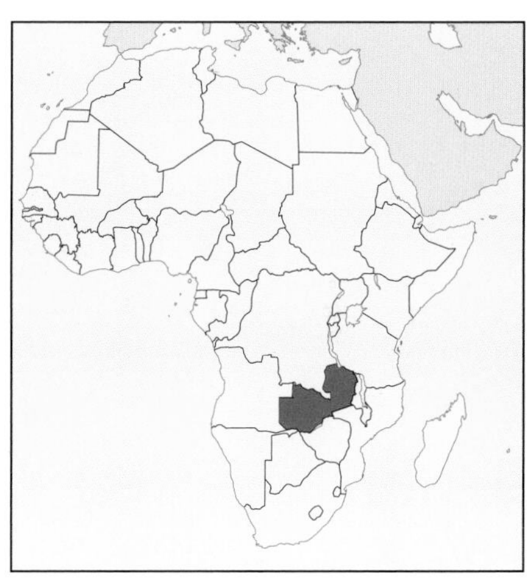

ZIMBABWE

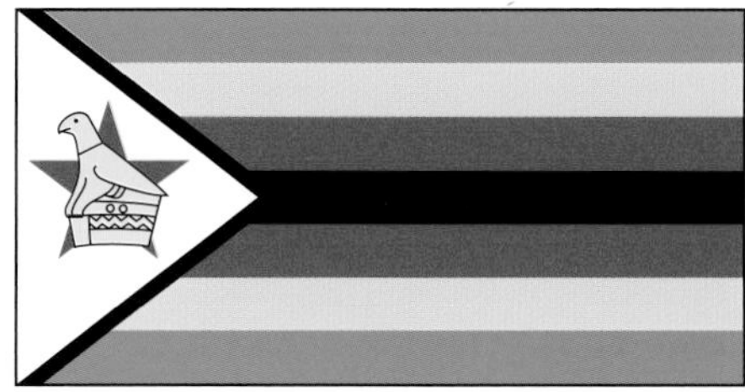

Facts and Figures

Capital: Harare 850,000 (1992)
Area (sq km): 390,000
Population: 10,700,000 (1992)
Language: English, Shona, Ndebele
Religion: Christian 53% Traditional
Currency: Zimbabwe Dollar = 100 cents
Annual Income per person: $620
Annual Trade per person: $381
Adult Literacy: 67%
Life Expectancy (F): 63
Life Expectancy (M): 59

Location Map

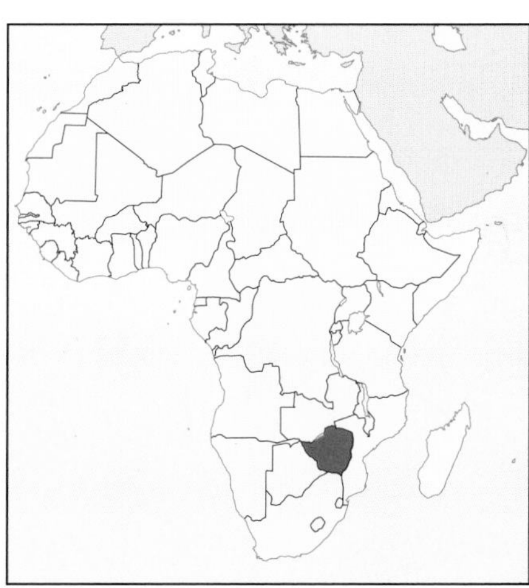

Flags of Asia

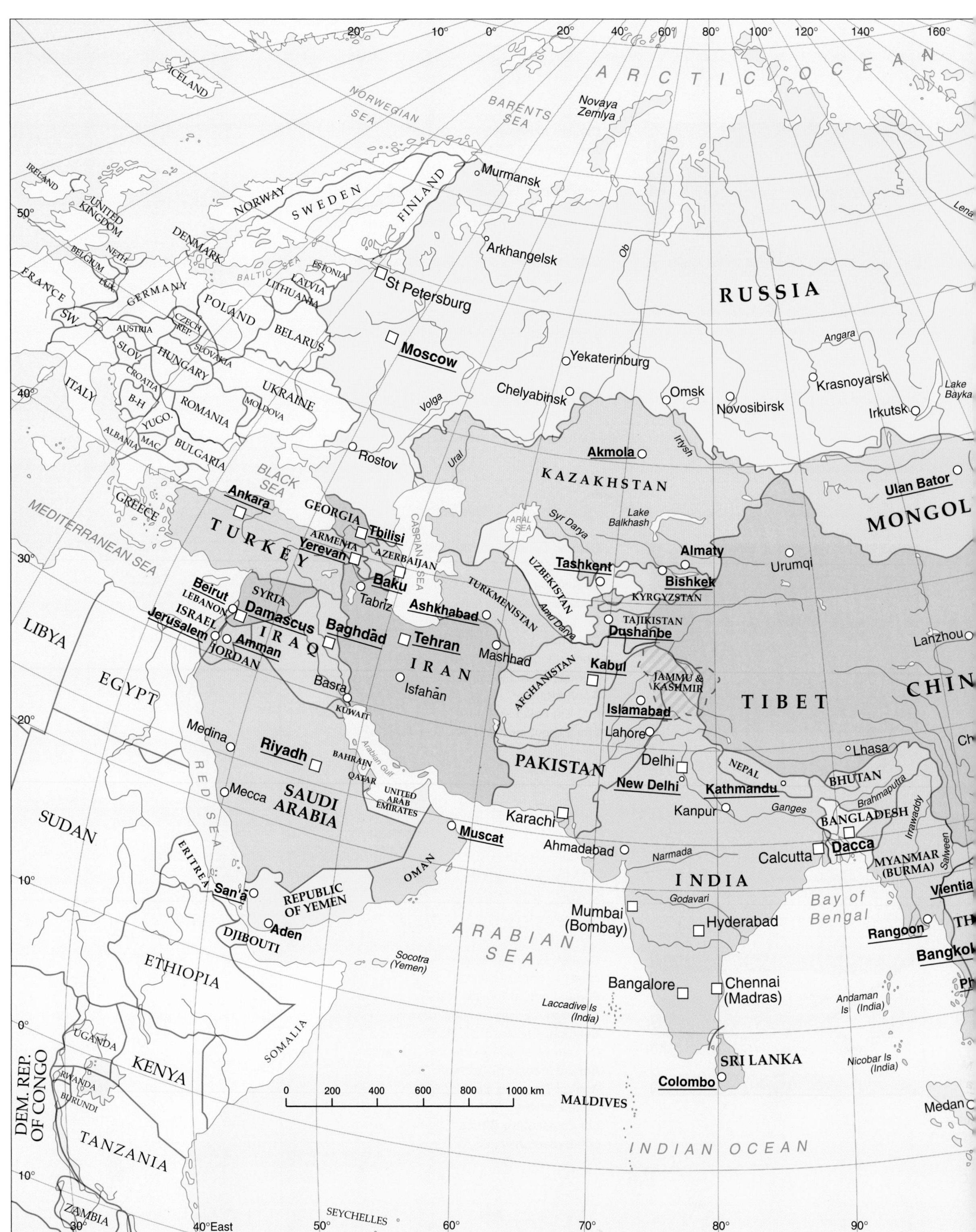

ASIA FLAG INDEX

Flags of Asia

AFGHANISTAN

Facts and Figures

Capital: Kabul 913,200 (1979)
Area (sq km): 652,090
Population: 16,560,000 (1990)
Language: Pushtu, Dari
Religion: Sunni Muslim 70% Shiite Muslim 25%
Currency: Afghani = 100 puls
Annual Income per person: $450
Annual Trade per person: $73
Adult Literacy: 30%
Life Expectancy (F): 44
Life Expectancy (M): 43

Location Map

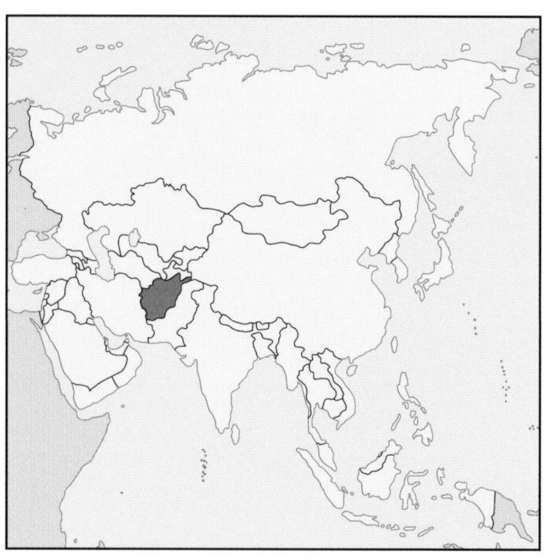

ARMENIA

Facts and Figures

Capital: Yerevan 1,185,000 (1990)
Area (sq km): 29,800
Population: 3,400,000 (1992)
Language: Armenian
Religion: Armenian Orthodox
Currency: Dram
Annual Income per person: $2,150
Annual Trade per person: $500
Adult Literacy: 93%
Life Expectancy (F): 73
Life Expectancy (M): 78

Location Map

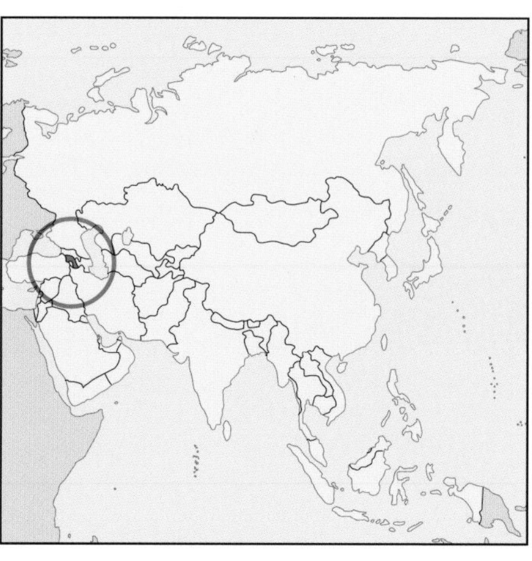

AZERBAIJAN

Facts and Figures

Capital: Baku 1,149,000 (1990)
Area (sq km): 86,600
Population: 7,200,000 (1992)
Language: Azerbaijani
Religion: Shiite Muslim 62% Sunni Muslim 26%
Currency: Manat
Annual Income per person: $1,670
Annual Trade per person: $400
Adult Literacy: 93%
Life Expectancy (F): 75
Life Expectancy (M): 67

Location Map

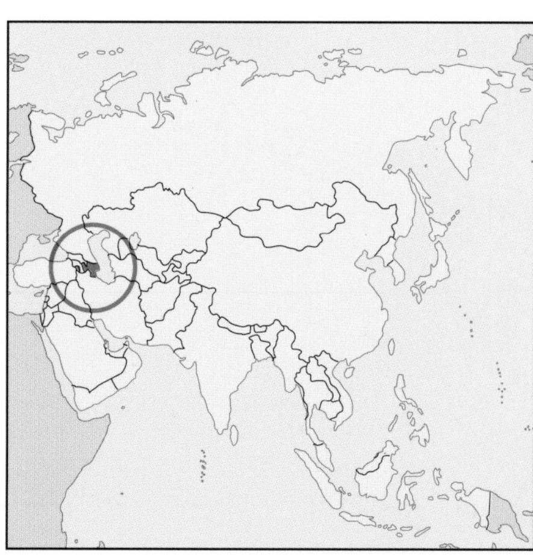

BAHRAIN

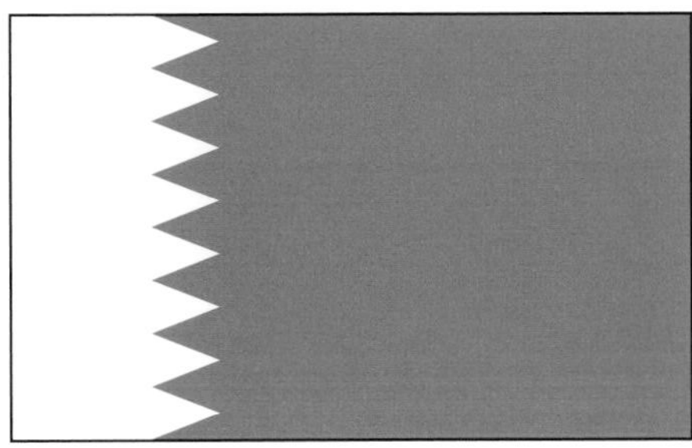

Facts and Figures

Capital: Manama 152,000 (1988)
Area (sq km): 688
Population: 538,000 (1993)
Language: Arabic
Religion: Shiite Muslim 60% Sunni Muslim 25% Christian 7%
Currency: Bahrain Dinar = 1000 fils
Annual Income per person: $6,910
Annual Trade per person: $14,094
Adult Literacy: 77%
Life Expectancy (F): 74
Life Expectancy (M): 70

Location Map

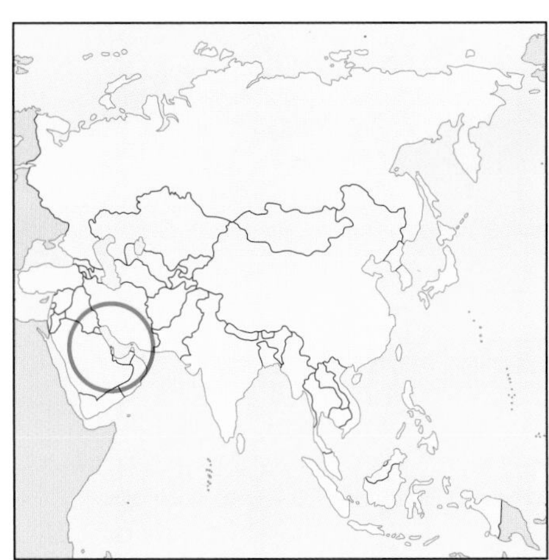

BANGLADESH

Facts and Figures

Capital: Dhaka 3,397,200 (1991)
Area (sq km): 148,400
Population: 118,700,000 (1993)
Language: Bengali, English
Religion: Sunni Muslim 85% Hindu 12%
Currency: Taka = 100 paisa
Annual Income per person: $220
Annual Trade per person: $43
Adult Literacy: 35%
Life Expectancy (F): 53
Life Expectancy (M): 53

Location Map

BHUTAN

Facts and Figures

Capital: Thimphu 30,340 (1993)
Area (sq km): 46,500
Population: 600,000 (1990)
Language: Tibetan, Nepalese
Religion: Buddhist 65% Hindu 33%
Currency: Ngultrum = 100 chetrum
Annual Income per person: $468
Annual Trade per person: Data not available
Adult Literacy: 35%
Life Expectancy (F): 49
Life Expectancy (M): 51

Location Map

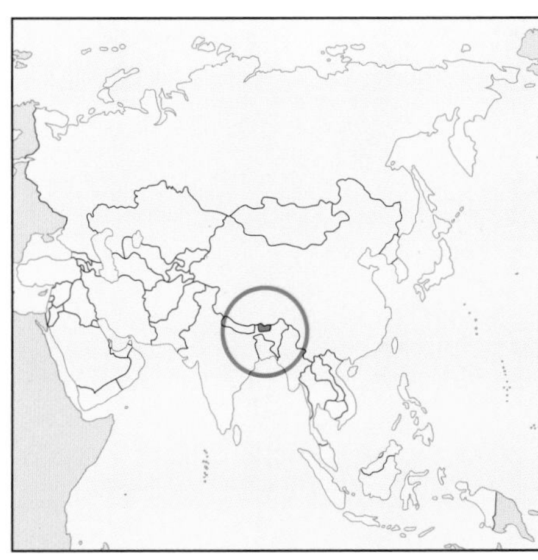

Flags of Asia

BRUNEI

Facts and Figures

Capital: Bandar Seri Begawan 45,870 (1991)
Area (sq km): 5,770
Population: 267,800 (1992)
Language: Malay, English, Chinese
Religion: Muslim 67% Buddhist 13% Christian10%
Currency: Brunei Dollar
Annual Income per person: $15,390
Annual Trade per person: $11,108
Adult Literacy: 86%
Life Expectancy (F): 77
Life Expectancy (M): 74

Location Map

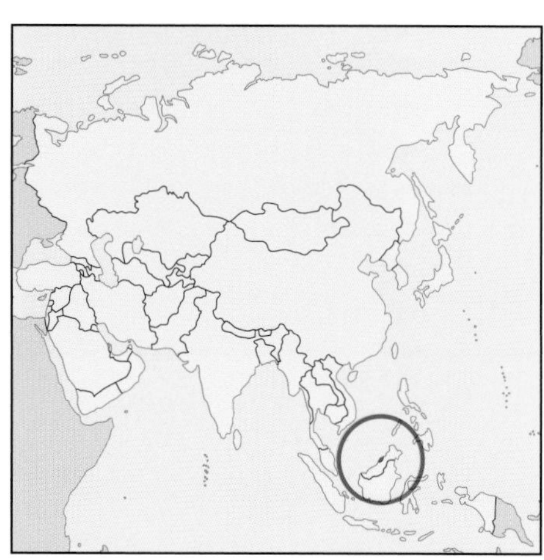

CAMBODIA

Facts and Figures

Capital: Phnom Penh 800,000 (1989)
Area (sq km): 181,040
Population: 12,000,000 (1993)
Language: Khmer ,French
Religion: Buddhist 88%
Currency: Riel = 100 sen
Annual Income per person: $200
Annual Trade per person: $25
Adult Literacy: 35%
Life Expectancy (F): 52
Life Expectancy (M): 50

Location Map

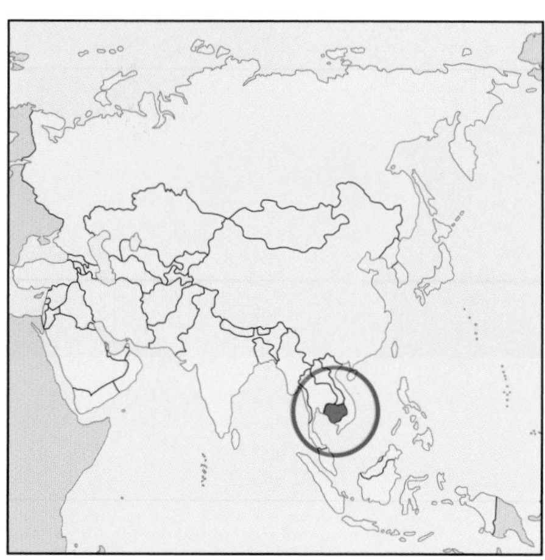

CHINA

Facts and Figures

Capital: Beijing 7,050,000 (1992)
Area (sq km): 9,560,000
Population: 1,158,000,000 (1992)
Language: Chinese
Religion: Confucian 20% Buddhist 6% Taoist 2% Muslim 2%
Currency: Renminbi yuan = 10jiao = 100fen
Annual Income per person: $370
Annual Trade per person: $137
Adult Literacy: 70%
Life Expectancy (F): 73
Life Expectancy (M): 69

Location Map

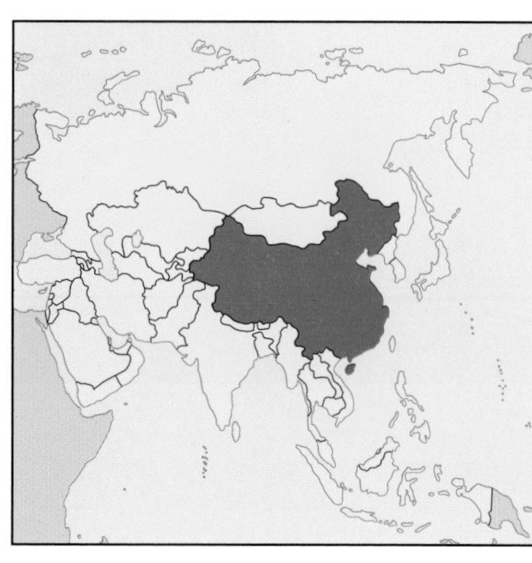

TAIWAN

Facts and Figures

Capital: Taipei 2,720,000 (1992)
Area (sq km): 36,100
Population: 20,600,000 (1991)
Language: Mandarin, Chinese
Religion: Buddhist 30% Taoist 18% Christian 4%
Currency: New Taiwan Dollar = 100 cents
Annual Income per person: $8,815
Annual Trade per person: $7,395
Adult Literacy: 91%
Life Expectancy (F): 77
Life Expectancy (M): 72

Location Map

GEORGIA

Facts and Figures

Capital: Tbilisi 1,283,000(1991)
Area (sq km): 69,700
Population: 5,460,000 (1990)
Language: Georgian, Armenian,Russian
Religion: Orthodox 83% Muslim 11%
Currency: Rouble = 100 kopeks
Annual Income per person: $1,640
Annual Trade per person: $300
Adult Literacy: Data not available
Life Expectancy (F): 76
Life Expectancy (M): 69

Location Map

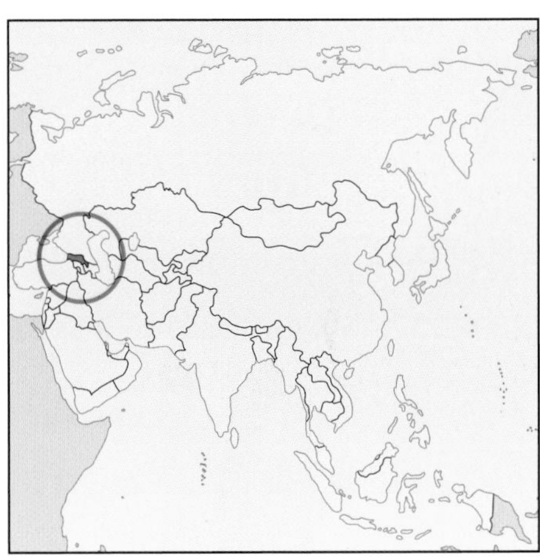

INDIA

Facts and Figures

Capital: New Delhi 7,508,000 (1991)
Area (sq km): 3,165,600
Population: 903,000,000 (1991)
Language: Hindi, English, Teluga, Bengali, Marati, Urdu
Religion: Hindu 83% Muslim 11% Christian 2% Sikh 2% Buddhist 1%
Currency: Rupee = 100 paisa
Annual Income per person: $330
Annual Trade per person: $44
Adult Literacy: 48%
Life Expectancy (F): 61
Life Expectancy (M): 60

Location Map

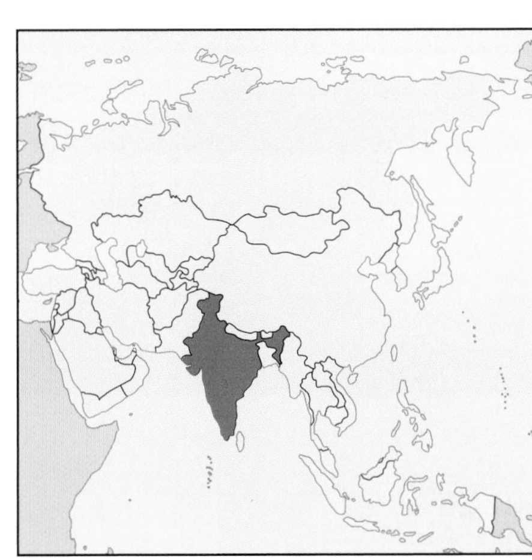

Flags of Asia

INDONESIA

Facts and Figures

Capital: Jakarta 9,000,000 (1993)
Area (sq km): 1,919,440
Population: 187,800,000 (1993)
Language: Bahasa Indonesian, Dutch
Religion: Sunni Muslim 87% Christian 9%
Currency: Rupiah = 100 sen
Annual Income per person: $620
Annual Trade per person: $293
Adult Literacy: 76%
Life Expectancy (F): 65
Life Expectancy (M): 61

Location Map

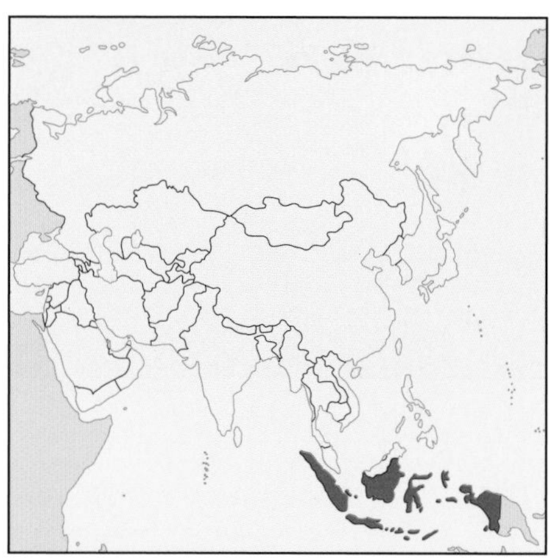

IRAN

Facts and Figures

Capital: Tehran 7,214,000 (1992)
Area (sq km): 1,648,000
Population: 61,600,000 (1992)
Language: Farsi, Kurdish, Baluchi
Religion: Shi'ite Muslim 94%
Currency: Rial = 100 dinars
Annual Income per person: $2,320
Annual Trade per person: $598
Adult Literacy: 54%
Life Expectancy (F): 68
Life Expectancy (M): 67

Location Map

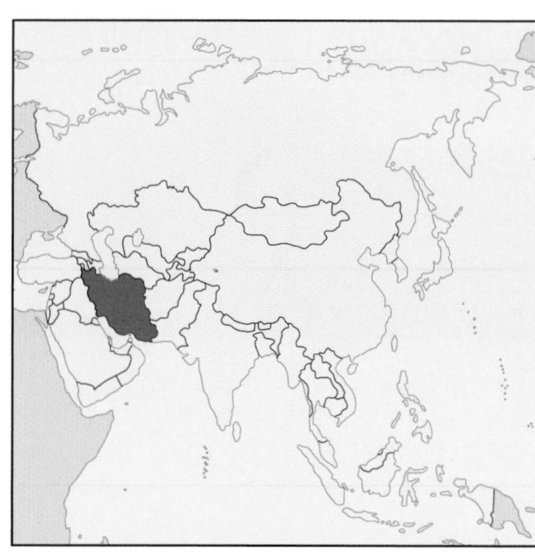

IRAQ

Facts and Figures

Capital: Baghdad 4,914,000 (1992)
Area (sq km): 438,320
Population: 19,410,000 (1993)
Language: Arabic, Kurdish, Turkish
Religion: Shi'ite Muslim 61%
Sunni Muslim 34%
Currency: Dinar = 20 dirhams
Annual Income per person: $2,100
Annual Trade per person: $276
Adult Literacy: 60%
Life Expectancy (F): 67
Life Expectancy (M): 65

Location Map

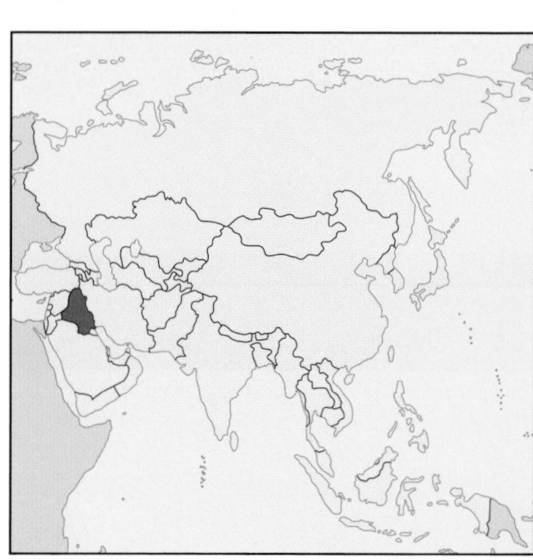

ISRAEL

Facts and Figures

Capital: Jerusalem 556,500 (1991)
Area (sq km): 27,010
Population: 7,200,000
Language: Hebrew, Arabic, English
Religion: Jewish 78% Muslim 13% Christian 2%
Currency: Shekel = 100 agorot
Annual Income per person: $11,330
Annual Trade per person: $5,794
Adult Literacy: 96%
Life Expectancy (F): 78
Life Expectancy (M): 74

Location Map

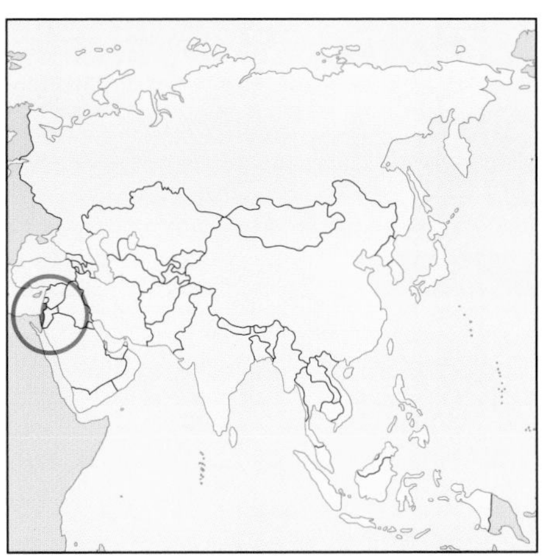

JAPAN

Facts and Figures

Capital: Tokyo 7,976,000 (1992)
Area (sq km): 377,750
Population: 124,900,000 (1992)
Language: Japanese,Korean,Chinese
Religion: Shintoism, Buddhism
Currency: Yen = 100 sen
Annual Income per person: $29,794
Annual Trade per person: $4,617
Adult Literacy: 99%
Life Expectancy (F): 82
Life Expectancy (M): 76

Location Map

JORDAN

Facts and Figures

Capital: Amman 1,272,000 (1992)
Area (sq km): 97,740
Population: 4,010,000 (1992)
Language: Arabic
Religion: Sunni Muslim 95% Christian 5%
Currency: Jordanian Dinar = 1000 fils
Annual Income per person: $1,120
Annual Trade per person: $825
Adult Literacy: 80%
Life Expectancy (F): 70
Life Expectancy (M): 66

Location Map

Flags of Asia

NORTH KOREA

Facts and Figures

Capital: Pyongyang 2,567,000 (1992)
Area (sq km): 122,762
Population: 22,030,000 (1991)
Language: Korean, Chinese
Religion: Chondogyo 14% Traditional 14%
Buddhist 2% Christian 1%
Currency: North Korean Won = 100 chon
Annual Income per person: $1,100
Annual Trade per person: $200
Adult Literacy: 99%
Life Expectancy (F): 72
Life Expectancy (M): 66

Location Map

SOUTH KOREA

Facts and Figures

Capital: Seoul 10,268,000 (1990)
Area (sq km): 99,270
Population: 43,663,000 (1990)
Language: Korean
Religion: Buddhist 24% Protestant 16%
Roman Catholic 5% Confucian 2%
Currency: South Korean Won = 100 chon
Annual Income per person: $6,743
Annual Trade per person: $3,546
Adult Literacy: 96%
Life Expectancy (F): 73
Life Expectancy (M): 67

Location Map

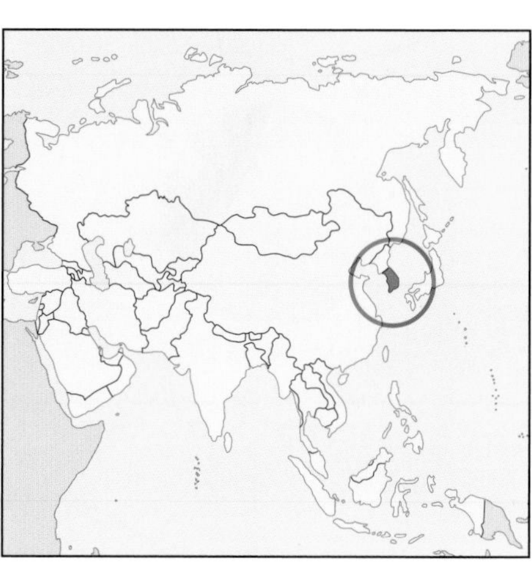

KAZAKHSTAN

Facts and Figures

Capital: Akmola 281,000 (1997)
Area (sq km): 2,717,300
Population: 17,200,000 (1992)
Language: Kazakh, Russian
Religion: Sunni Muslim,Christian
Currency: Tenge = 500 rubles
Annual Income per person: $2,470
Annual Trade per person: $500
Adult Literacy: Data not available
Life Expectancy (F): 73
Life Expectancy (M): 64

Location Map

KUWAIT

Facts and Figures

Capital: Kuwait City 31,300 (1993)
Area (sq km): 17,820
Population: 2,100,000 (1991)
Language: Arabic, English
Religion: Sunni Muslim 78%
Shiite Muslim 14% Christian 6%
Currency: Kuwaiti Dinar =1000 fils
Annual Income per person: $16,380
Annual Trade per person: $8,682
Adult Literacy: 74%
Life Expectancy (F): 77
Life Expectancy (M): 72

Location Map

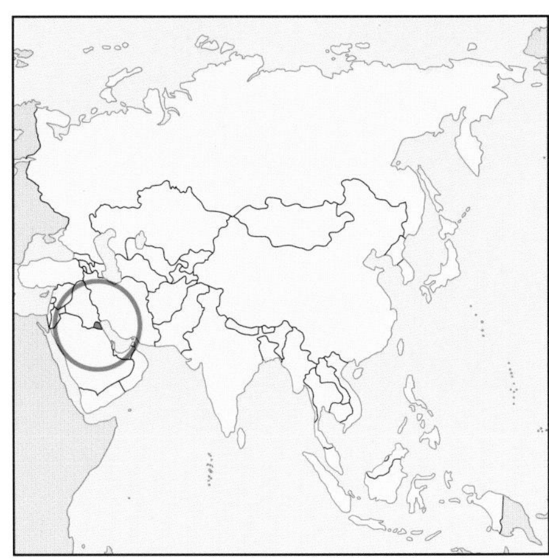

KYRGYZSTAN

Facts and Figures

Capital: Bishkek 641,400 (1991)
Area (sq km): 198,500
Population: 4,500,000 (1992)
Language: Kirghiz
Religion: Sunni Muslim,Christian
Currency: Som=100 tyiyn
Annual Income per person: $1,550
Annual Trade per person: $30
Adult Literacy: Data not available
Life Expectancy (F): 73
Life Expectancy (M): 65

Location Map

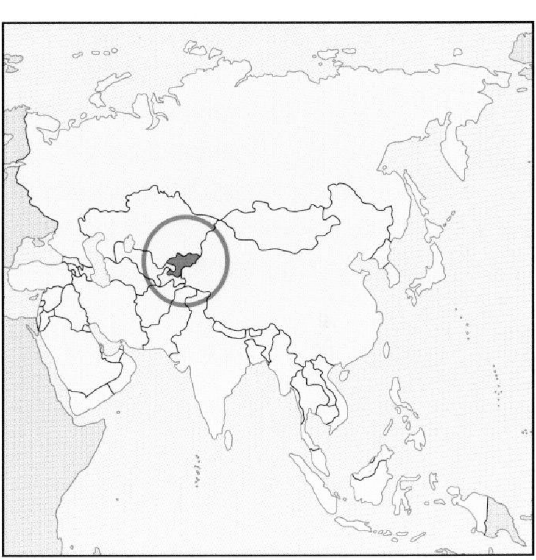

LAOS

Facts and Figures

Capital: Vientiane 454,000 (1992)
Area (sq km): 236,800
Population: 4,400,000 (1993)
Language: Lao, French, English
Religion: Buddhist 52% Traditional 33%
Currency: Kip = 100 cents
Annual Income per person: $230
Annual Trade per person: $62
Adult Literacy: 84%
Life Expectancy (F): 53
Life Expectancy (M): 50

Location Map

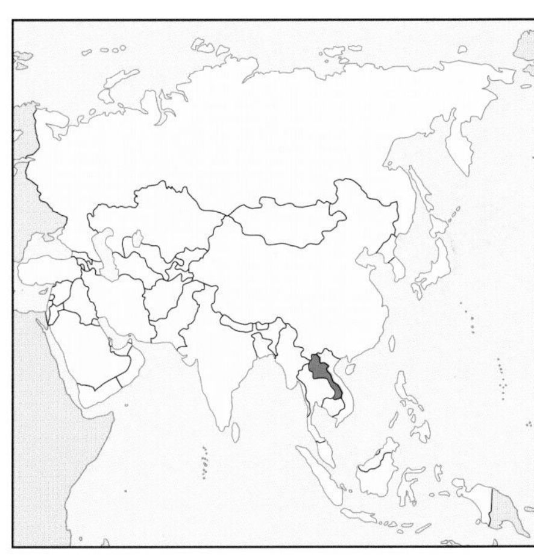

Flags of Asia

LEBANON

Facts and Figures

Capital: Beirut 1,500,000 (1992)
Area (sq km): 10,400
Population: 2,760,000 (1991)
Language: Arabic ,French, English, Armenian
Religion: Shi'ite Muslim 35% Maronite Christian 27% Sunni Muslim 23%
Currency: Lebanese Pound = 100 piastres
Annual Income per person: $2,000
Annual Trade per person: $750
Adult Literacy: 80%
Life Expectancy (F): 69
Life Expectancy (M): 65

Location Map

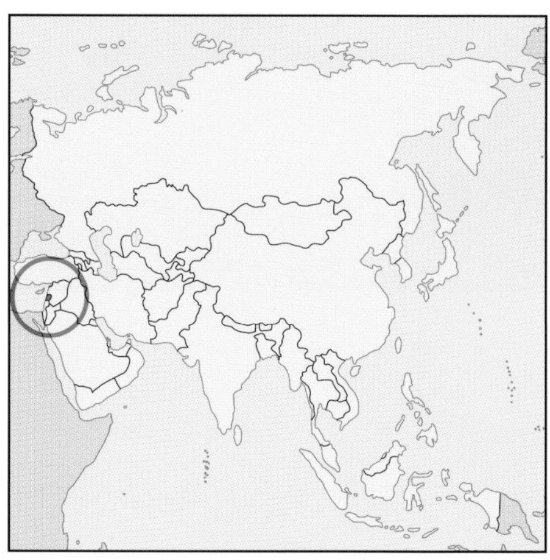

MALAYSIA

Facts and Figures

Capital: Kuala Lumpur 1,233,000 (1990)
Area (sq km): 329,760
Population: 19,030,000 (1993)
Language: Bahasa Malaysian, Chinese, Tamil, English
Religion: Sunni Muslim 53% Buddhist 17% Taoist,Hindu,Christian
Currency: Ringgit = 100 sen
Annual Income per person: $3,265
Annual Trade per person: $3,877
Adult Literacy: 79%
Life Expectancy (F): 73
Life Expectancy (M): 69

Location Map

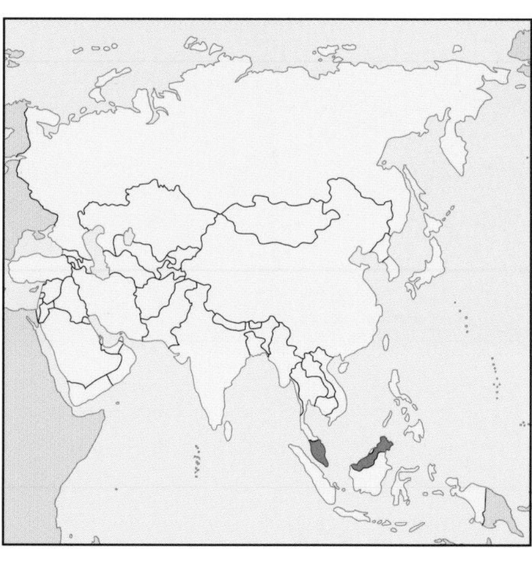

MALDIVES

Facts and Figures

Capital: Malé 55,130 (1990)
Area (sq km): 298
Population: 238,400 (1993)
Language: Divehi, English, Arabic
Religion: Sunni Muslim
Currency: Rufiyaa = 100 laari
Annual Income per person: $460
Annual Trade per person: $750
Adult Literacy: 92%
Life Expectancy (F): 63
Life Expectancy (M): 61

Location Map

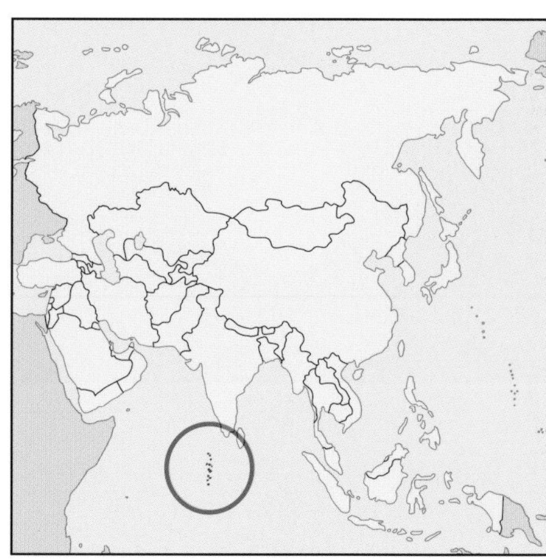

MONGOLIA

Facts and Figures

Capital: Ulan Bator 55,000 (1991)
Area (sq km): 1,566,500
Population: 2,260,000 (1992)
Language: Halh Mongol, Chinese, Russian
Religion: Shamanist 31% Muslim 4% Buddhist
Currency: Tugrik = 100 mongo
Annual Income per person: $600
Annual Trade per person: $400
Adult Literacy: 91%
Life Expectancy (F): 65
Life Expectancy (M): 62

Location Map

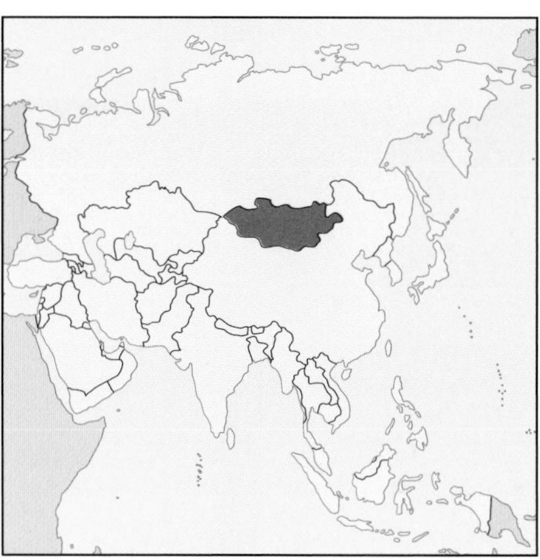

MYANMAR

Facts and Figures

Capital: Rangoon 2,458,710 (1983)
Area (sq km): 676,577
Population: 42,330,000 (1993)
Language: Burmese, English
Religion: Buddhist
Currency: Kyat=100pyas
Annual Income per person: $500
Annual Trade per person: $24
Adult Literacy: 81%
Life Expectancy (F): 64
Life Expectancy (M): 61

Location Map

NEPAL

Facts and Figures

Capital: Kathmandu 419,000 (1991)
Area (sq km): 147,200
Population: 19,360,000 (1991)
Language: Nepalese, Tibetan
Religion: Hindu 89% Buddhist 5%
Currency: Nepalese Rupee = 100 paisa
Annual Income per person: $180
Annual Trade per person: $54
Adult Literacy: 26%
Life Expectancy (F): 53
Life Expectancy (M): 54

Location Map

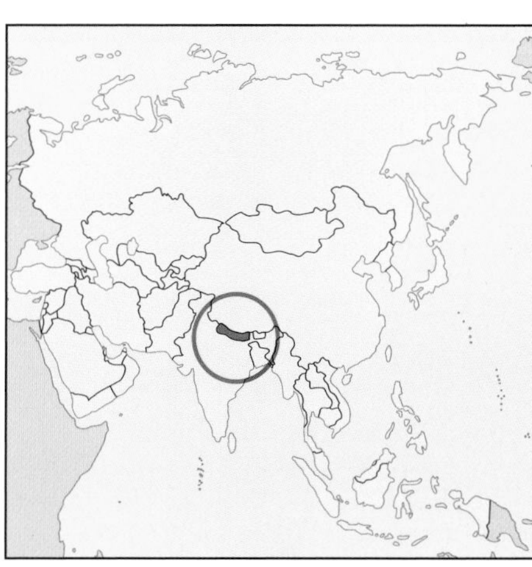

Flags of Asia

OMAN

Facts and Figures

Capital: Muscat 320,000 (1992)
Area (sq km): 309,500
Population: 2,070,000 (1991)
Language: Arabic, English, Baluchi
Religion: Muslim 86%
Currency: Omani Rial = 1000 baiza
Annual Income per person: $5,500
Annual Trade per person: $5,172
Adult Literacy: 35%
Life Expectancy (F): 70
Life Expectancy (M): 66

Location Map

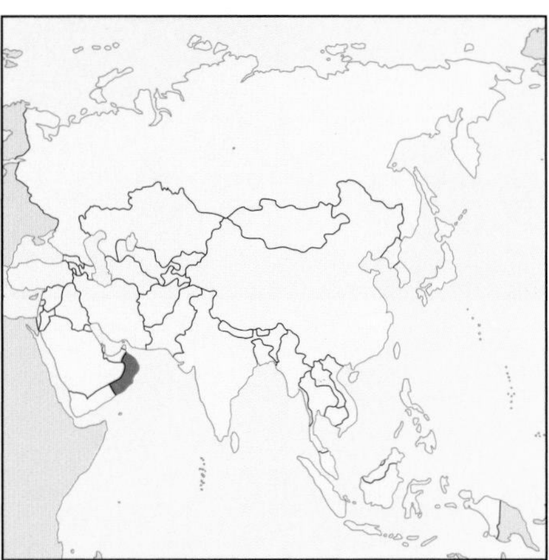

PAKISTAN

Facts and Figures

Capital: Islamabad 272,000 (1992)
Area (sq km): 796,100
Population: 122,400,000 (1992)
Language: Urdu, Punjabi, Sindhi, Baluchi, Pushtu, English
Religion: Muslim 96% Hindu, Christian
Currency: Pakistan Rupee = 100 paisa
Annual Income per person: $400
Annual Trade per person: $129
Adult Literacy: 35%
Life Expectancy (F): 59
Life Expectancy (M): 59

Location Map

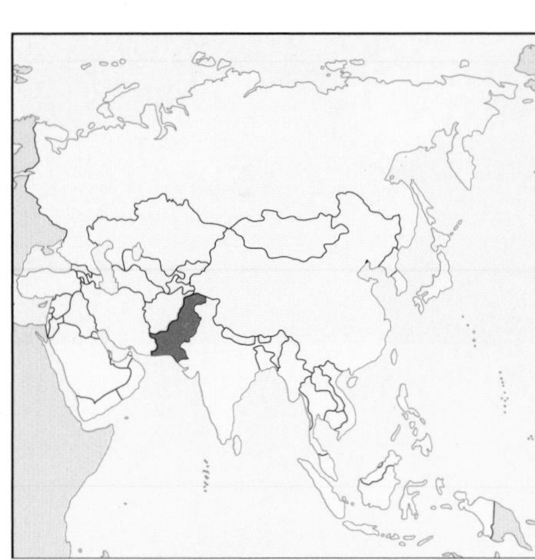

PHILIPPINES

Facts and Figures

Capital: Manila 1,599,000 (1990)
Area (sq km): 300,000
Population: 65,650,000 (1993)
Language: Pilipino, English
Religion: Roman Catholic 76% Protestant 5% Sunni Muslim 4%
Currency: Piso = 100 sentimos
Annual Income per person: $740
Annual Trade per person: $332
Adult Literacy: 90%
Life Expectancy (F): 70
Life Expectancy (M): 63

Location Map

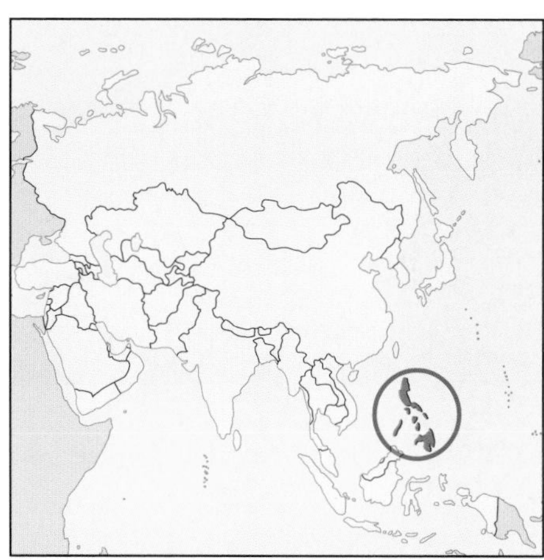

QATAR

Facts and Figures

Capital: Doha 286,000 (1992)
Area (sq km): 11,500
Population: 510,000
Language: Arabic
Religion: Sunni Muslim 92%
Currency: Qatari Riyal = 100 dirhams
Annual Income per person: $15,870
Annual Trade per person: $28,296
Adult Literacy: 82%
Life Expectancy (F): 73
Life Expectancy (M): 68

Location Map

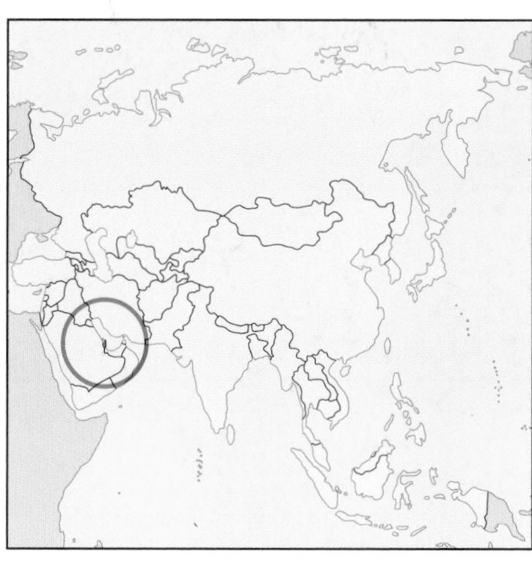

RUSSIA

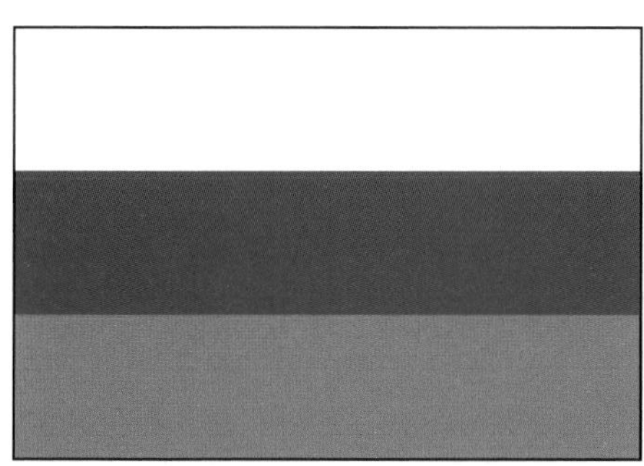

Facts and Figures

Capital: Moscow 8,967,000 (1990)
Area (sq km): 17,075,000
Population: 148,700,000 (1992)
Language: Russian
Religion: Orthodox 25% Muslim Buddhist
Currency: Rouble = 100 kopeks
Annual Income per person: $3,222
Annual Trade per person: $680
Adult Literacy: 94%
Life Expectancy (F): 74
Life Expectancy (M): 64

Location Map

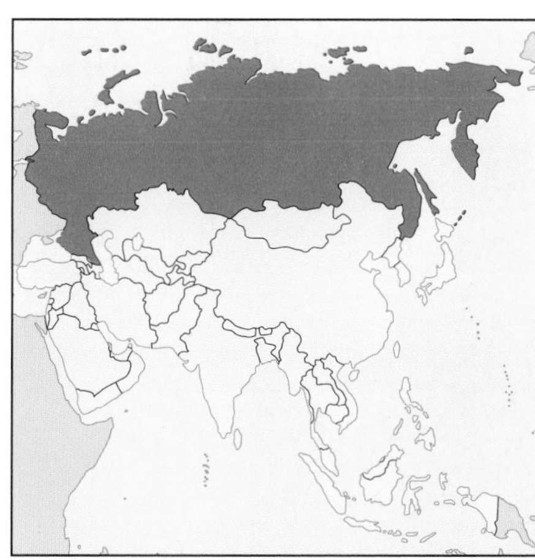

Flags of Asia

SAUDI ARABIA

Facts and Figures

Capital: Riyadh 2,320,000 (1992)
Area (sq km): 2,200,000
Population: 16,900,000 (1992)
Language: Arabic
Religion: Sunni Muslim 92% Shi'ite Muslim 8%
Currency: Rial = 100 halalas
Annual Income per person: $7,070
Annual Trade per person: $4,606
Adult Literacy: 62%
Life Expectancy (F): 68
Life Expectancy (M): 64

Location Map

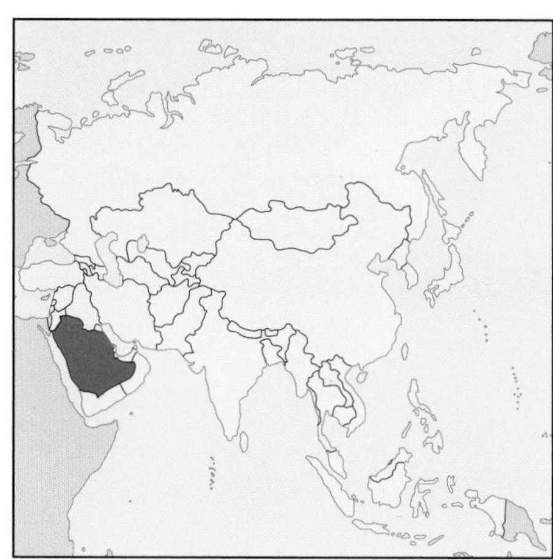

SINGAPORE

Facts and Figures

Capital: Singapore 2,820,000 (1992)
Area (sq km): 640
Population: 2,820,000 (1992)
Language: Chinese, Malay ,Tamil ,English
Religion: Buddhist 28% Taoist 13%
Christian 19% Muslim 16%
Hindu 5%
Currency: Singapore Dollar
Annual Income per person: $13,060
Annual Trade per person: $48,275
Adult Literacy: 88%
Life Expectancy (F): 77
Life Expectancy (M): 72

Location Map

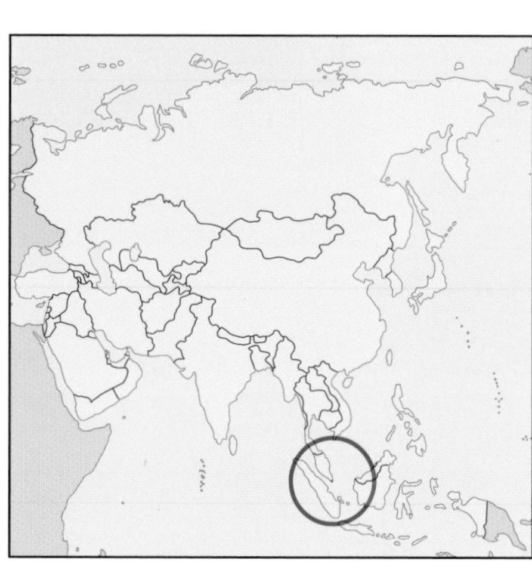

SRI LANKA

Facts and Figures

Capital: Colombo 615,000 (1990)
Area (sq km): 65,610
Population: 17,400,000 (1992)
Language: Sinhala, Tamil, English
Religion: Buddhist 64% Hindu 13% Muslim 8%
Christian 7%
Currency: Sri Lankan Rupee = 100 cents
Annual Income per person: $539
Annual Trade per person: $293
Adult Literacy: 88%
Life Expectancy (F): 74
Life Expectancy (M): 70

Location Map

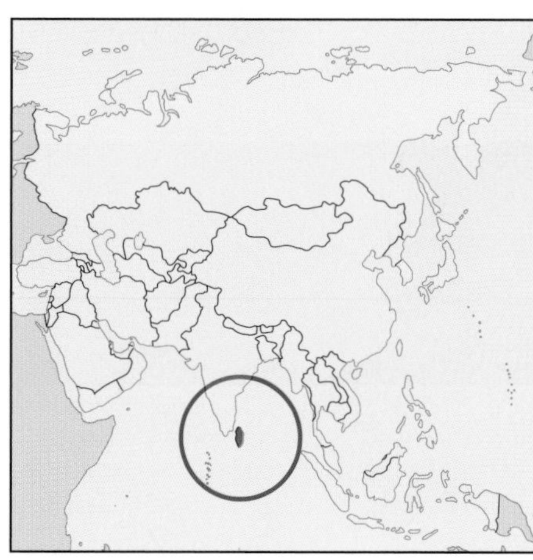

SYRIA

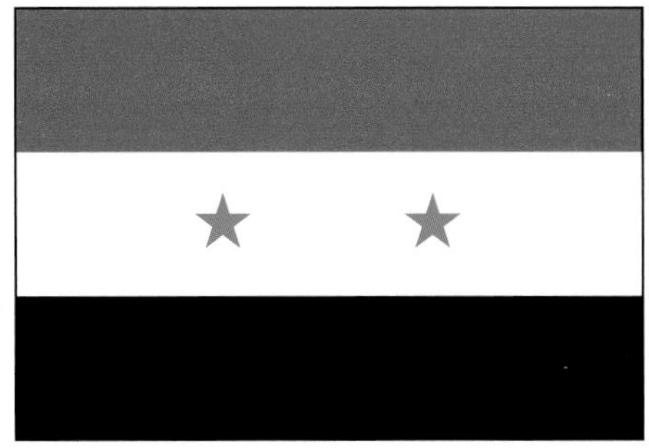

Facts and Figures

Capital: Damascus 1,450,000 (1993)
Area (sq km): 185,180
Population: 13,400,000 (1993)
Language: Arabic, Kurdish, Armenian
Religion: Sunni Muslim 90% Christian 9%
Currency: Syrian Pound = 100 piastres
Annual Income per person: $1, 100
Annual Trade per person: $502
Adult Literacy: 64%
Life Expectancy (F): 69
Life Expectancy (M): 65

Location Map

TAJIKISTAN

Facts and Figures

Capital: Dushanbe 592,000 (1991)
Area (sq km): 143,100
Population: 5,500,000(1993)
Language: Tajik ,Uzbek, Russian
Religion: Sunni Muslim
Currency: Rouble =100 kopecks
Annual Income per person: $1,050
Annual Trade per person: $400
Adult Literacy: Data not available
Life Expectancy (F): 72
Life Expectancy (M): 67

Location Map

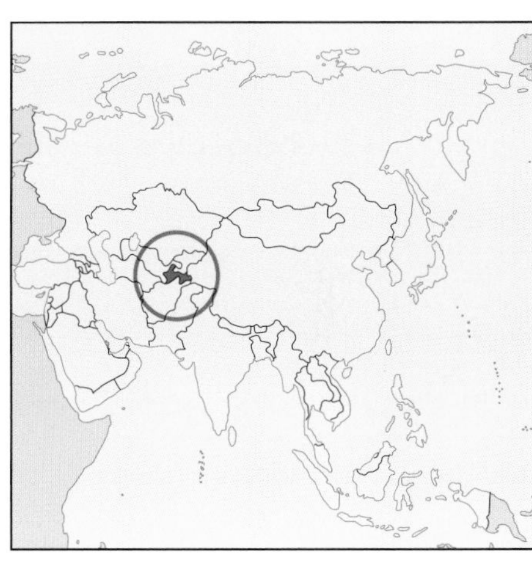

THAILAND

Facts and Figures

Capital: Bangkok 5,876,000 (1990)
Area (sq km): 513,115
Population: 57,800,000 (1993)
Language: Thai, Lao, Chinese, Malay
Religion: Buddhist 94% Muslim 4%
Currency: Baht = 100 satang
Annual Income per person: $1,580
Annual Trade per person: $1,152
Adult Literacy: 93%
Life Expectancy (F): 69
Life Expectancy (M): 65

Location Map

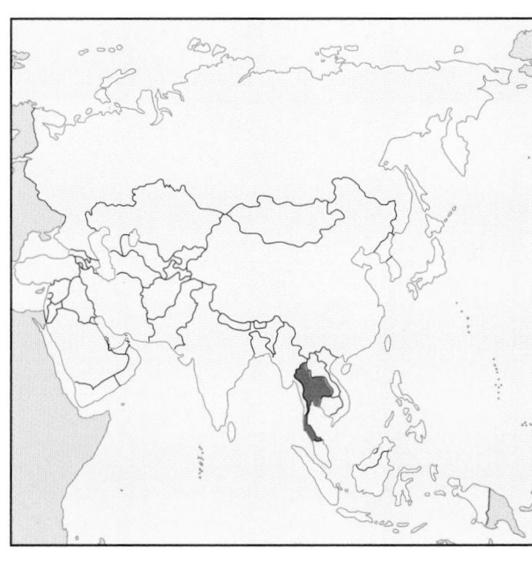

Flags of Asia

TURKMENISTAN

Facts and Figures

Capital: Ashkhabad 411,000 (1990)
Area (sq km): 488,100
Population: 3,800,000 (1992)
Language: Turkmen, Russian
Religion: Muslim 85%
Currency: Manat
Annual Income per person: $1,700
Annual Trade per person: $350
Adult Literacy: Data not available
Life Expectancy (F): 70
Life Expectancy (M): 63

Location Map

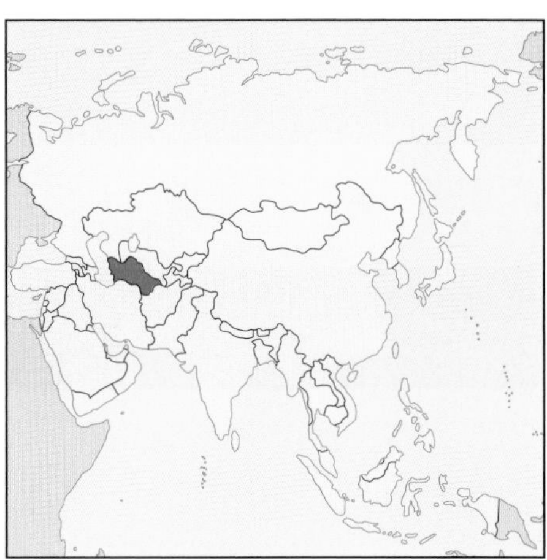

UNITED ARAB EMIRATES

Facts and Figures

Capital: Abu Dhabi 806,000 (1992)
Area (sq km): 83,657
Population: 2,100,000 (1993)
Language: Arabic ,English
Religion: Sunni Muslim 96%
Currency: Dirham = 100 fils
Annual Income per person: $19,870
Annual Trade per person: $19,745
Adult Literacy: 55%
Life Expectancy (F): 74
Life Expectancy (M): 70

Location Map

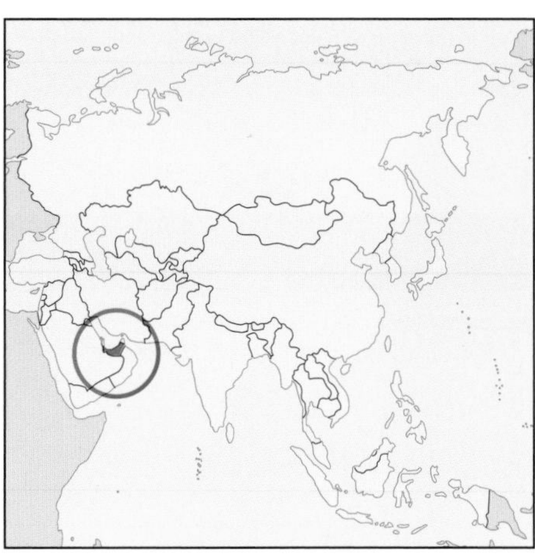

UZBEKISTAN

Facts and Figures

Capital: Tashkent 2,115,000 (1991)
Area (sq km): 447,400
Population: 21,200,000 (1992)
Language: Uzbek, Russian, Tajik
Religion: Sunni Muslim 75%
Currency: Rouble = 100 kopeks
Annual Income per person: $1,350
Annual Trade per person: $250
Adult Literacy: 93%
Life Expectancy (F): 73
Life Expectancy (M): 66

Location Map

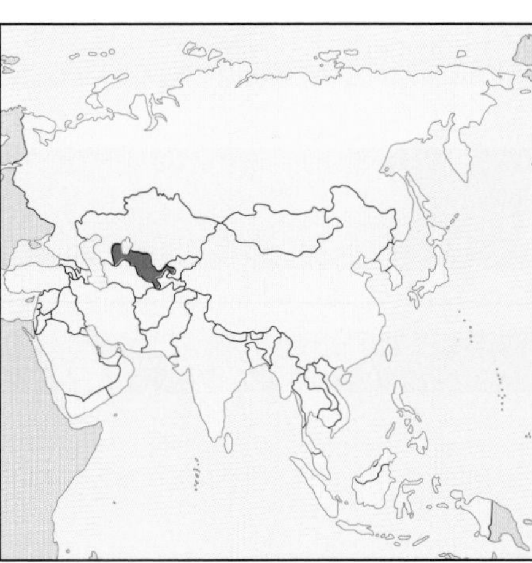

VIETNAM

Facts and Figures

Capital: Hanoi 2,100,000 (1992)
Area (sq km): 329,570
Population: 69,300,000 (1992)
Language: Vietnamese
Religion: Buddhist 52% Roman Catholic 7%
Taoist
Currency: Dong = 10 hao
Annual Income per person: $300
Annual Trade per person: $60
Adult Literacy: 88%
Life Expectancy (F): 66
Life Expectancy (M): 62

Location Map

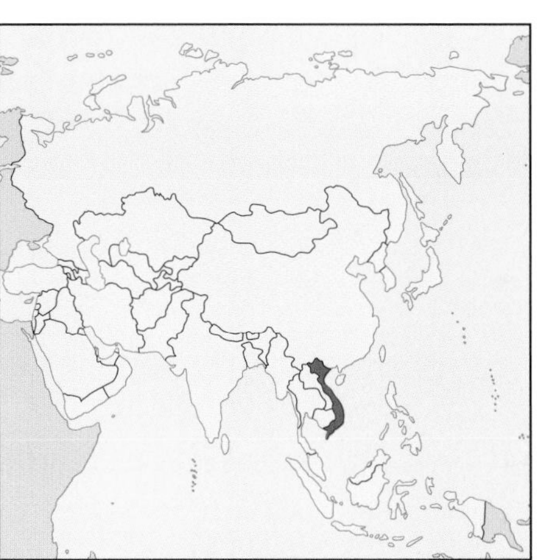

YEMEN

Facts and Figures

Capital: San'a 500,000 (1990)
Area (sq km): 531,000
Population: 13,000,000 (1993)
Language: Arabic
Religion: Sunni Muslim 45%
Shi'ite Muslim 41%
Currency: N Yemeni Riyal and
S Yemeni Dinar
Annual Income per person: $540
Annual Trade per person: $141
Adult Literacy: 39%
Life Expectancy (F): 52
Life Expectancy (M): 52

Location Map

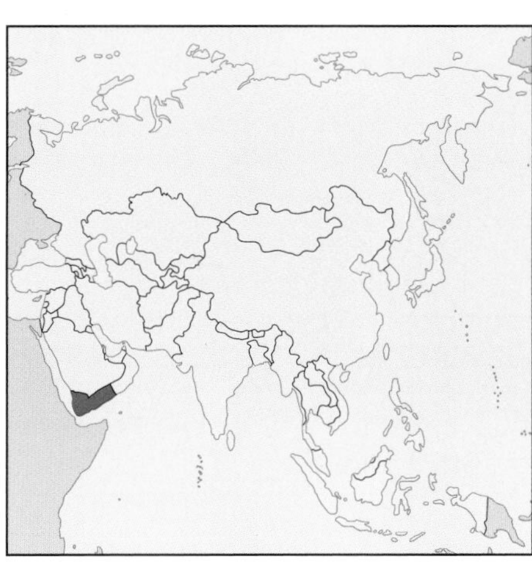

Flags of Oceania

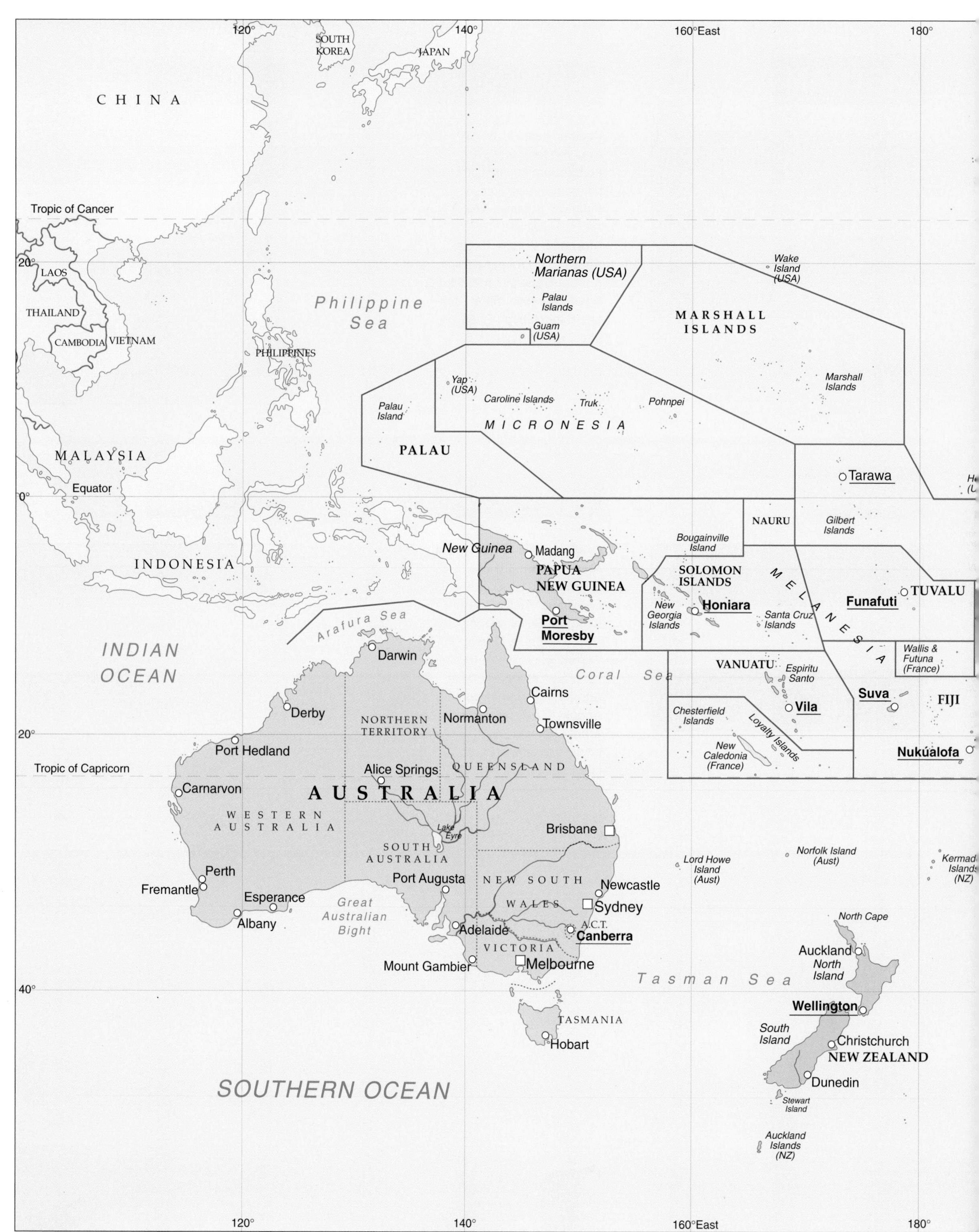

Flags of Oceania

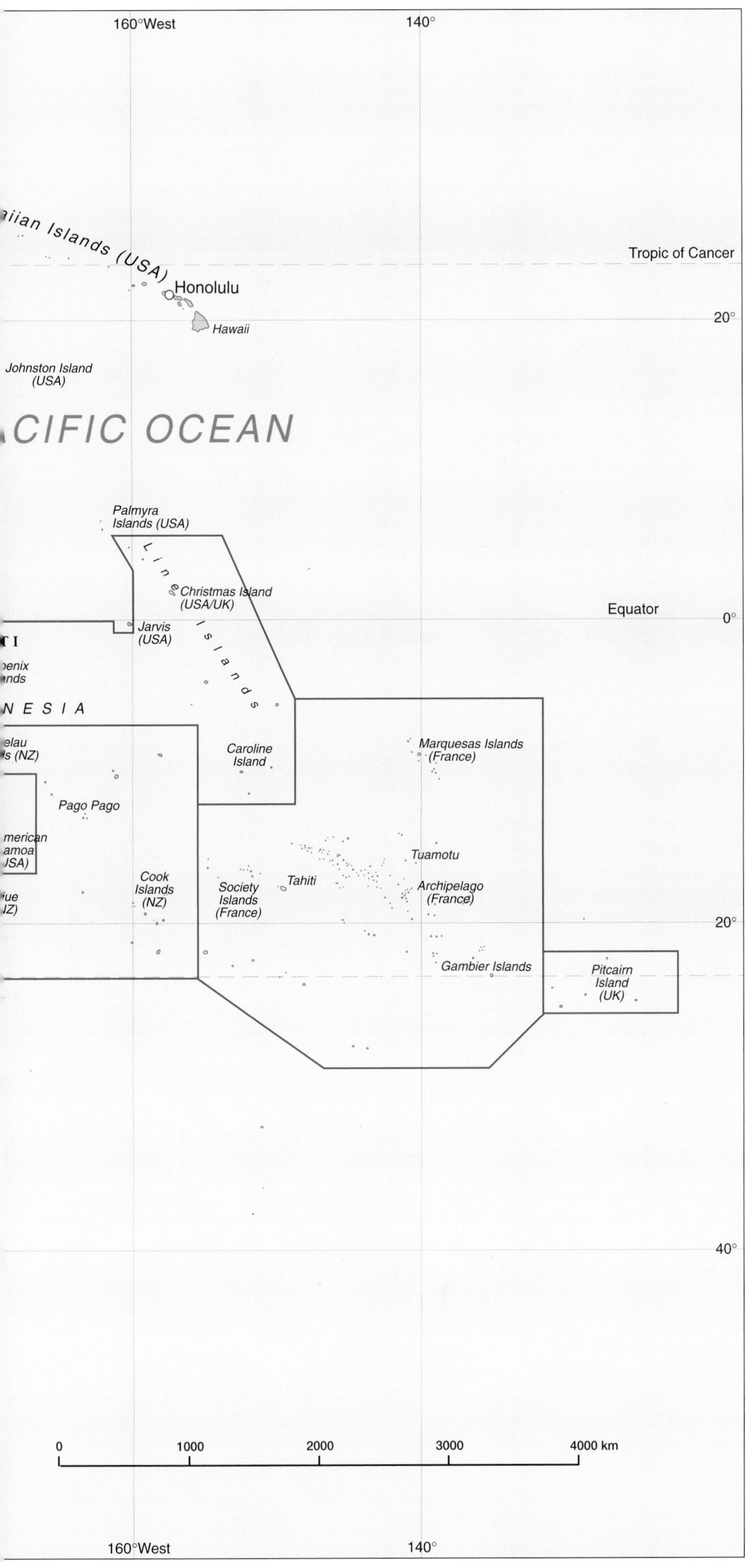

OCEANIA FLAG INDEX

Flags of Oceania

AUSTRALIA

Facts and Figures

Capital: Canberra 278,000 (1991)
Area (sq km): 7,682,300
Population: 17,500,000 (1992)
Language: English
Religion: Catholic 26% Anglican 24%
Other Christian 16%
Currency: Australian Dollar
Annual Income per person: $16,590
Annual Trade per person: $4,741
Adult Literacy: 99%
Life Expectancy (F): 80
Life Expectancy (M): 74

Location Map

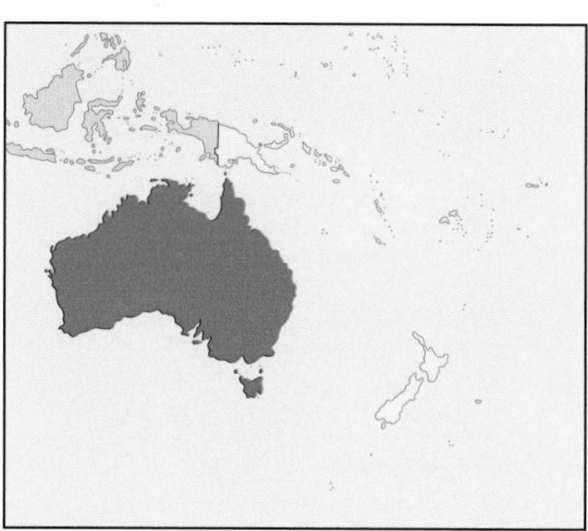

COOK ISLANDS

Facts and Figures

Capital: Avarua
Area (sq km): 240
Population: 18,000
Language: English
Religion: Christian 69% Roman Catholic 15%
Currency: Cook Island Dollar
Annual Income per person: Data not available
Annual Trade per person: Data not available
Adult Literacy: Data not available
Life Expectancy (F): Data not available
Life Expectancy (M): Data not available

Location Map

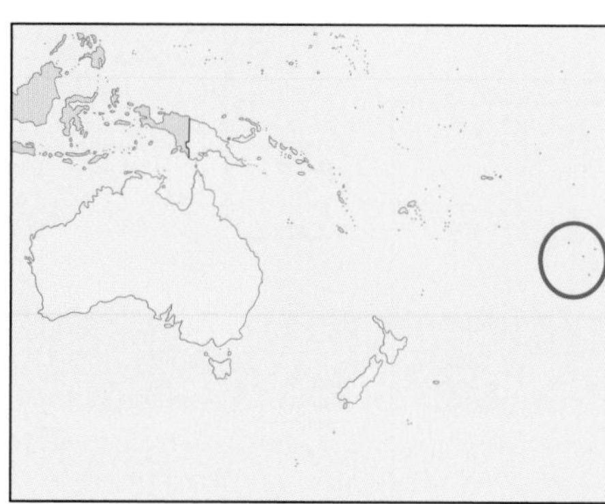

FIJI

Facts and Figures

Capital: Suva 73,500 (1992)
Area (sq km): 18,333
Population: 758,275 (1993)
Language: English,Bauan,Hindustani
Religion: Christian 50% Hindu 36%
Muslim 7%
Currency: Fiji dollar = 100 cents
Annual Income per person: $1,830
Annual Trade per person: $1,491
Adult Literacy: 87%
Life Expectancy (F): 68
Life Expectancy (M): 64

Location Map

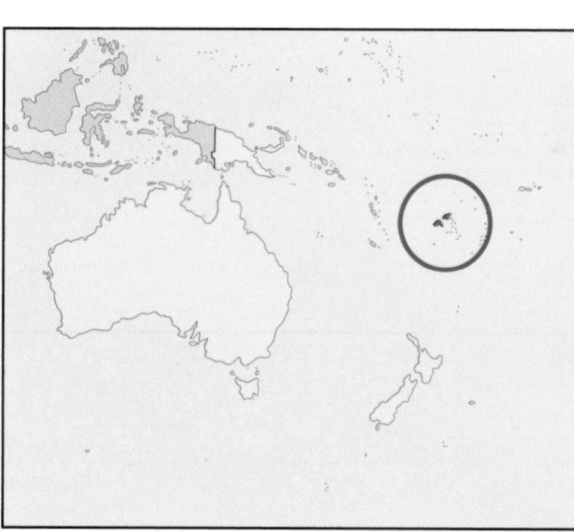

FRENCH POLYNESIA

Facts and Figures

Capital: Papeete
Area (sq km): 4,000
Population: 210,000
Language: French, Tahitian
Religion: Protestant 54% Roman Catholic 30%
Currency: CFP Franc
Annual Income per person: $6,000
Annual Trade per person: $4,500
Adult Literacy: 98%
Life Expectancy (F): 71
Life Expectancy (M): 66

Location Map

KIRIBATI

Facts and Figures

Capital: Kiribati 25,200 (1990)
Area (sq km): 720
Population: 72,300 (1991)
Language: English, Gilbertese
Religion: Roman Catholic 53% Protestant 39%
Currency: Australian Dollar
Annual Income per person: $750
Annual Trade per person: $350
Adult Literacy: Data not available
Life Expectancy (F): 58
Life Expectancy (M): 52

Location Map

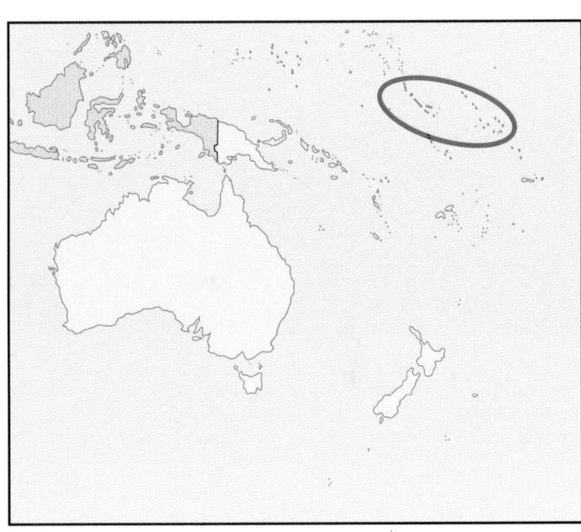

NORTHERN MARIANAS

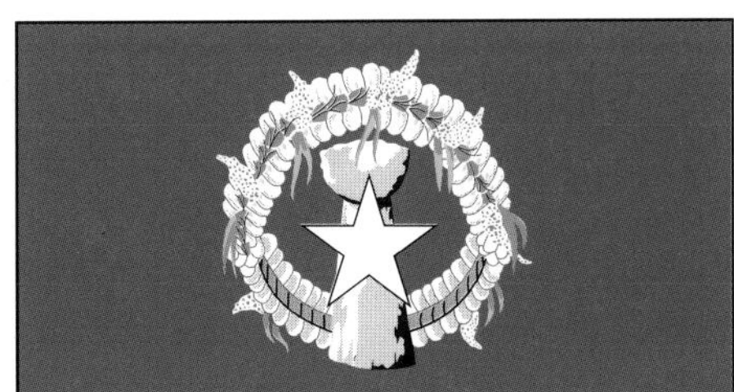

Facts and Figures

Capital: Saipan 38,900 (1990)
Area (sq km): 477
Population: 45.200 (1991)
Language: English, Chamorro
Religion: Roman Catholic
Currency: US Dollar
Annual Income per person: $3,500
Annual Trade per person: $10,000
Adult Literacy: 96%
Life Expectancy (F): 70
Life Expectancy (M): 65

Location Map

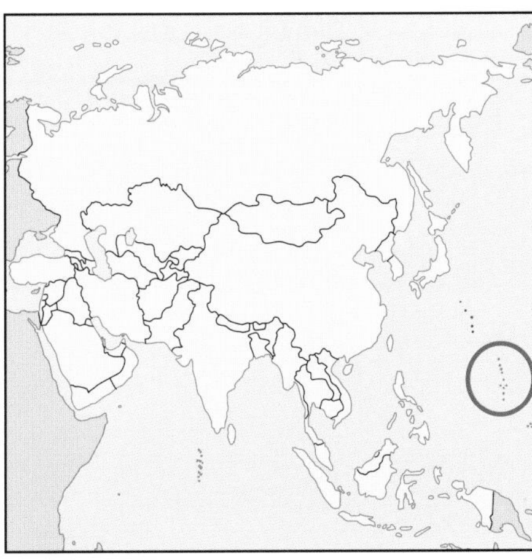

Flags of Oceania

MARSHALL ISLANDS

Facts and Figures

Capital: Dalap-Uliga-Darrit 20,000 (1990)
Area (sq km): 181
Population: 45,600 (1990)
Language: Marshallese, English
Religion: Protestant
Currency: US Dollar
Annual Income per person: $1,500
Annual Trade per person: $700
Adult Literacy: 93%
Life Expectancy (F): 64
Life Expectancy (M): 61

Location Map

MICRONESIA

Facts and Figures

Capital: Kolonia
Area (sq km): 703
Population: 107,900 (1990)
Language: English
Religion: Christian
Currency: US Dollar
Annual Income per person: $1,500
Annual Trade per person: $700
Adult Literacy: 78%
Life Expectancy (F): 73
Life Expectancy (M): 68

Location Map

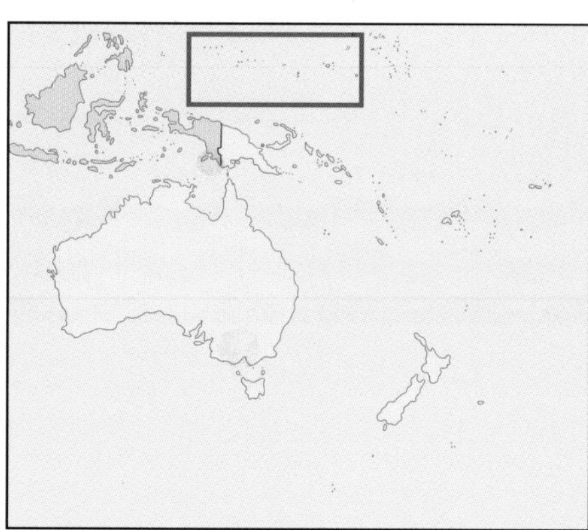

NAURU

Facts and Figures

Capital: Yaren 7,500 (1990)
Area (sq km): 21
Population: 8,100 (1990)
Language: English,Nauruan
Religion: Roman Catholic, Protestant
Currency: Australian Dollar
Annual Income per person:$10,000
Annual Trade per person: $18,000
Adult Literacy: Data not available
Life Expectancy (F): 69
Life Expectancy (M): 64

Location Map

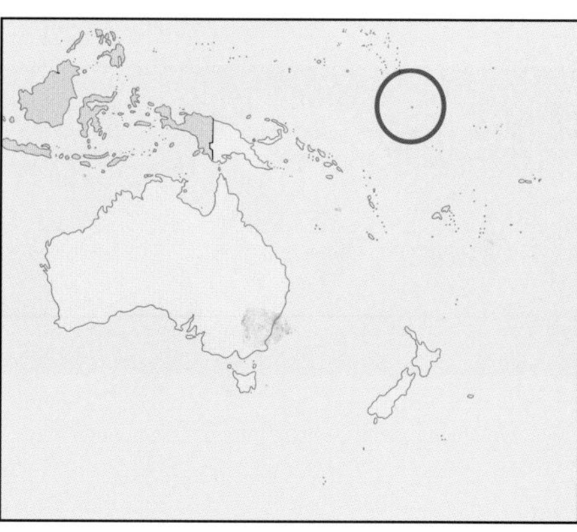

NEW ZEALAND

Facts and Figures

Capital: Wellington 325,700 (1992)
Area (sq km): 270,530
Population: 3,495,000 (1993)
Language: English,Maori
Religion: Protestant 44% Roman Catholic 14% Other 7%
Currency: New Zealand Dollar
Annual Income per person: $12,140
Annual Trade per person: $5,615
Adult Literacy: 99%
Life Expectancy (F): 79
Life Expectancy (M): 73

Location Map

NIUE

Facts and Figures

Capital: Alofi 682 (1991)
Area (sq km): 260
Population: 2,239
Language: English, Niuean
Religion: Christian
Currency: New Zealand Dollar
Annual Income per person: Data not available
Annual Trade per person: Data not available
Adult Literacy: Data not available
Life Expectancy (F): Data not available
Life Expectancy (M): Data not available

Location Map

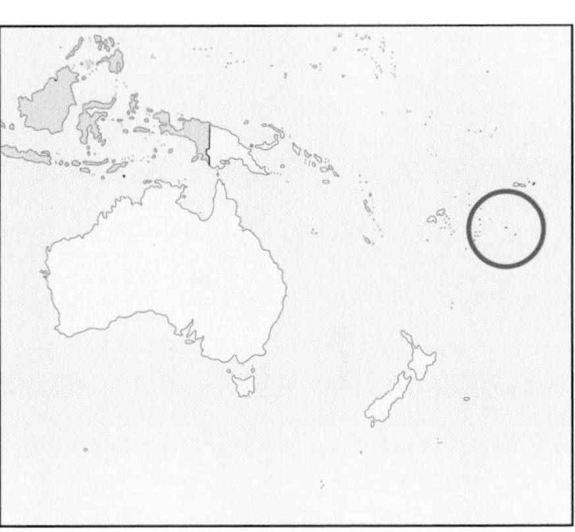

PALAU

Facts and Figures

Capital: Koror 10,500 (1990)
Area (sq km): 488
Population: 15,200 (1990)
Language: Palaun,English
Religion: Roman Catholic
Currency: US Dollar
Annual Income per person: $2,550
Annual Trade per person: $1,922
Adult Literacy: Data not available
Life Expectancy (F): 74
Life Expectancy (M): 68

Location Map

Flags of Oceania

SOLOMON ISLANDS

Facts and Figures

Capital: Honiara 33,800 (1989)
Area (sq km): 28,400
Population: 349,500 (1993)
Language: English, various Melanesian, Papuan and Polynesian languages
Religion: Protestant 75% Roman Catholic 19%
Currency: Solomon Island Dollar = 100 cents
Annual Income per person: $560
Annual Trade per person: $506
Adult Literacy: 24%
Life Expectancy (F): 72
Life Expectancy (M): 67

Location Map

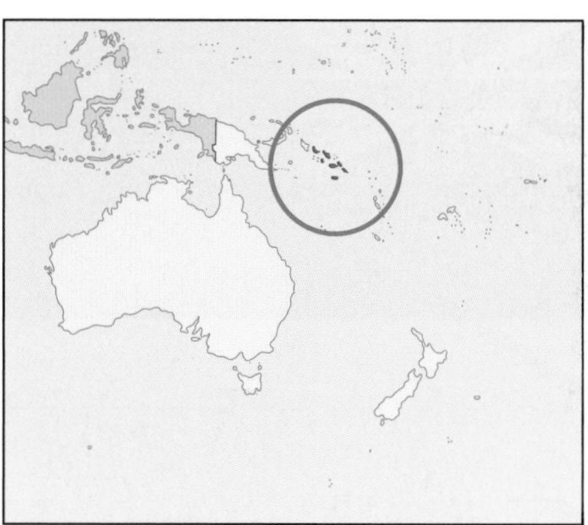

TONGA

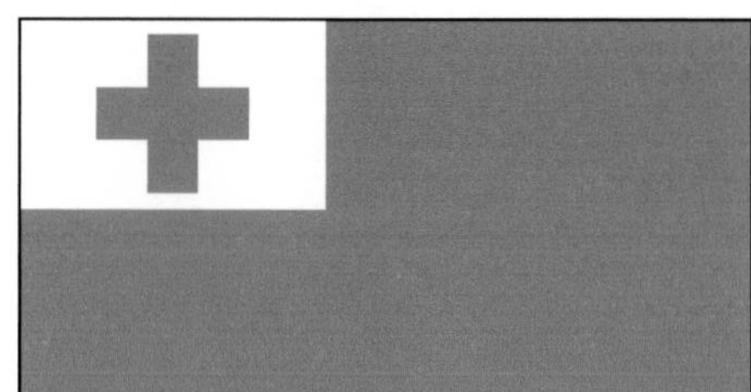

Facts and Figures

Capital: Nuku'alofa 29,000 (1986)
Area (sq km): 748
Population: 103,000 (1991)
Language: Tongan, English
Religion: Protestant 39%
Currency: Pa'anga = 100 seniti
Annual Income per person: $1,100
Annual Trade per person: $811
Adult Literacy: 99%
Life Expectancy (F): 70
Life Expectancy (M): 65

Location Map

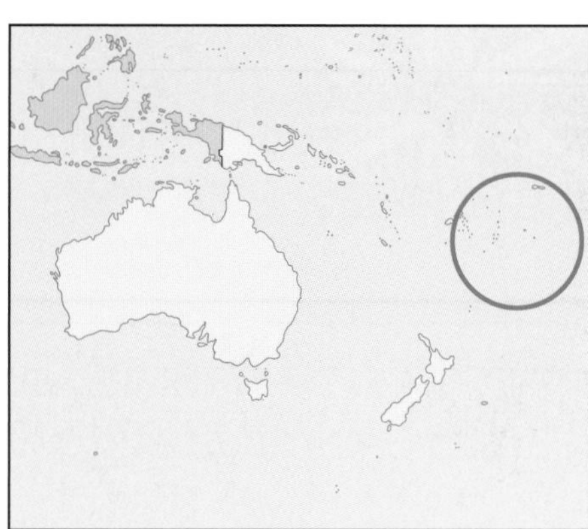

TUVALU

Facts and Figures

Capital: Funafuti 3,100 (1992)
Area (sq km): 24
Population: 10,090 (1991)
Language: Tuvaluan, English
Religion: Christian
Currency: Australian Dollar
Annual Income per person: $550
Annual Trade per person: $400
Adult Literacy: 95%
Life Expectancy (F): 63
Life Expectancy (M): 61

Location Map

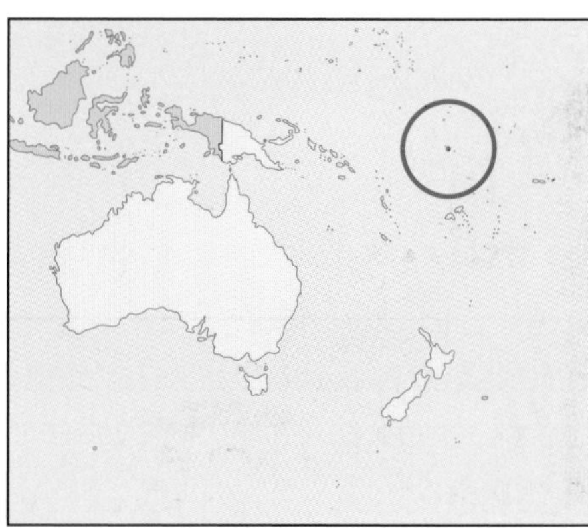

VANUATU

Facts and Figures

Capital: Port-Vila 19,400 (1989)
Area (sq km): 12,190
Population: 154,000 (1992)
Language: Bislama, English, French
Religion: Christian
Currency: Vatu = 100 centimes
Annual Income per person: $1,120
Annual Trade per person: $644
Adult Literacy: 67%
Life Expectancy (F): 72
Life Expectancy (M): 67

Location Map

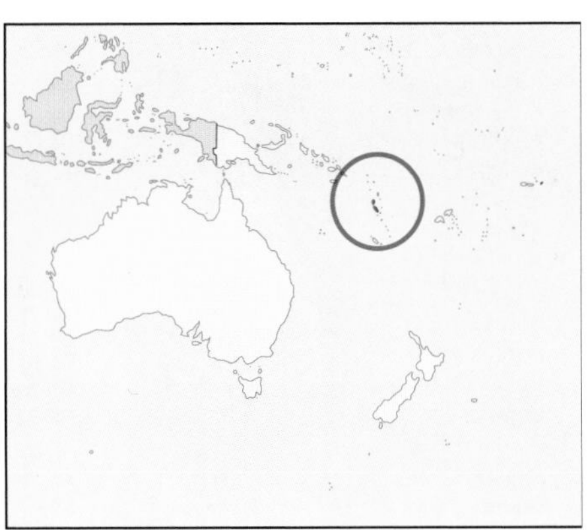

SAMOA

Facts and Figures

Capital: Apia 32,200 (1986)
Area (sq km): 2,830
Population: 168,000 (1990)
Language: Samoan, English
Religion: Protestant 62% Roman Catholic 22%
Currency: Tala = 100 sene
Annual Income per person: $930
Annual Trade per person: $629
Adult Literacy: 92%
Life Expectancy (F): 69
Life Expectancy (M): 64

Location Map

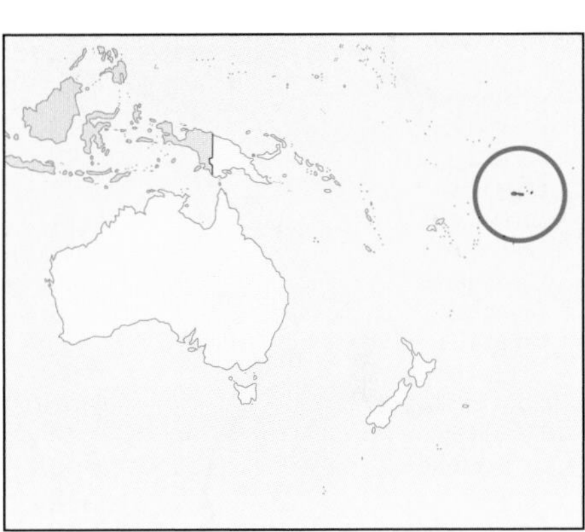

PAPUA NEW GUINEA

Facts and Figures

Capital: Port Moresby 193,300 (1990)
Area (sq km): 462,840
Population: 3,850,000 (1992)
Language: English, Aira Motu, Pidgin
Religion: Protestant 56% Roman Catholic 31% Traditional
Currency: Kina = 100 toea
Annual Income per person: $820
Annual Trade per person: $712
Adult Literacy: 52%
Life Expectancy (F): 57
Life Expectancy (M): 55

Location Map

Index